CYPRIAN OF CARTHAGE

AND THE UNITY OF THE CHRISTIAN CHURCH

Peter Hinchliff

Fellow of Balliol College, Oxford

GEOFFREY CHAPMAN

Geoffrey Chapman Publishers
An imprint of Cassell and Collier
Macmillan Publishers Ltd.
35 Red Lion Square, London WC1R 4SG
and at Sydney, Auckland, Toronto,
Johannesburg
an affiliate of Macmillan
Inc. New York

ISBN 0 225 66035 0

First published 1974

Made and printed in Great Britain by
The Camelot Press Ltd, Southampton

Contents

For my Father

Introductory Note

I have to confess that I have written this book largely for fun.
Early Church history has never been my special field, but I have
always been fascinated by the character and personality of
Cyprian and dissatisfied with the way he is usually represented.
Some years ago I wrote a biography of a nineteenth-century
bishop and it occurred to me that it would be interesting to
apply the same sort of techniques to a life of Cyprian. After all,
a fairly large number of his letters survive, as well as several
books which he wrote. One could treat these as if they were the
newly discovered correspondence and literary remains of any
eminent bishop and see what sort of figure emerged. It has not,
of course, been possible to ignore entirely what has already been
said about Cyprian, but I have tried, as far as possible, to read
and use his letters simply as a collection of letters and to let
them form their own picture for me. In attempting to tell the
story I have treated the resultant picture simply as fact, instead
of arguing in the text for and against every possible hypothesis.
I have tried, as far as my knowledge and ability allow, to
thrash out the hypotheses for myself, but it did not seem proper
to tell the story of a man's life in the jerky, discursive manner
which is inevitable if one stops to argue the precise dating of
each event and the precise text of each piece of writing. One
would not do this with a nineteenth-century subject, unless it
were vital to some crucial point in his life. This is the sort of rule
I have tried to follow. The specialist will find the result very

inadequate and unsatisfying. But it has been a fascinating exercise and, I hope, a kite worth flying.

Abbreviations used in References

Benson E. W. Benson, *Cyprian: his Life, his Times, his Work,* Macmillan, London, 1897

Frend W. H. C. Frend, *The Donatist Church,* Clarendon Press, Oxford, 1952

PL J. P. Migne, *Patrologia Latina,* with volume and column number

Cyprian's Epistles

English readers are likely to come across Cyprian's letters in four principal editions, two in the original and two in translation. They are Migne's *Patrologia Latina,* the Vienna *Corpus Scriptorum Ecclesiasticorum Latinorum* (CSEL), the so-called Oxford edition published by Henry Parker in 1844, and the volume edited by R. E. Wallis in the Ante-Nicene Christian Library. All these were published in the nineteenth century. CSEL is rather later than Migne and slightly better, though far from entirely satisfactory. Unfortunately the four editions do not use the same numbering for the epistles. Oxford and CSEL use one system, and Migne another. A-NCL follows Migne for the first twenty-two letters and then varies slightly. I have decided to use the CSEL/Oxford numbering, which is that used by Benson and by most modern writers, but for the convenience of readers who may wish to consult the English text of A-NCL or the Latin of Migne, a comparative table of the numbering of the epistles is provided at the end of the book. I have based my own translation on that of Wallis in A-NCL.

Acknowledgment

I am most grateful to the Clarendon Press and to the Reverend Maurice Bévenot, S.J., for permission to quote the translation of Cyprian's *De Unitate* from the edition of *De Lapsis and De Ecclesiae Catholicae Unitate* in the Oxford Early Christian Texts series.

1

It was mid-September in the year 258. For most of the day the headless body of a convicted criminal, leader of a dangerous subversive movement, had been lying on an open patch of ground outside the city. His execution had been public, and the public—his own followers and the general populace—had been urged by the authorities to be present. The idea had been, of course, to discourage the equally subversive tendencies of others by showing them the punishment they were likely to receive. It had not quite worked like that. There had, indeed, been one nasty moment when the body fell and there was blood everywhere and someone in the crowd yelled, 'We will die with him.' But the moment passed and, for some reason, the chief note of the day had been one of curious peace and quiet.

The body lay there in the humid heat. Small groups of people moved out from the crowd and came to look at the dead man. His closest friends and followers stood round. They had made no pretence of being disinterested. They kept watch and were unmolested. Their views were like his and they were known. Why the authorities left them free was something of a mystery. But if they could stand there, others could pass by the spot. So they came. The first few were, no doubt, other disciples. But there were sightseers, too, and the sadistic seekers of entertainment, the curious, those whom he had helped when they were poor and plague-stricken, those who had followed his career with admiration, those who had known him well before the days of his notoriety. They came and looked, and moved on. Before long the whole thing had the appearance of a solemn lying-in-state.

In the distance were the great mountains, becoming bluer as the day wore on. Here, where the corpse lay, the land was hollowed like a saucer. Rich red earth, vivid, raw-looking, had been tended, cultivated, made into gardens for the wealthy. Here were villas and orchards and vineyards. A ring of trees stood round the shallow depression and the incongruous body and the crowds. And on the dusty road to the city little groups of people came and went all day.

The city was on the coast, built on hills overlooking the sea, so that the land rose as one came out of the plain and then fell again, more steeply. The earth became greyer, more sandy, as it met the waters. On top of the hills were the crowded, over-heated, noisy little streets of the city, filled with the buzz of gossip and the excited movement of the crowds. In the public baths, this execution would be the great subject for conversation. It was the culmination of a long series of events stretching back nearly ten years. A prominent public figure had joined an undesirable religious sect. Not made for obscurity, he had become its local leader within a matter of months. When the sect was outlawed, his behaviour had been, at first, rather dubious. He had run away. The proletariat had bayed for his blood in the streets and he, who had been a rigid disciplinarian with others, had not been able or willing to face the test himself. He had spent a year as a fugitive and then come back to the city when the penalties were once more in abeyance. Again he was a prominent figure, less of a martinet, charitable, affable, dignified. He was the acknowledged 'father' of the Christians. He was said to be prominent among even the other leaders of the sect in the western world. Then there had been another period of crisis. This time he had not tried to escape. And he was dead.

As it became dusk the day cooled a little, though it was only when one was exposed to the sea breeze that the used-up atmosphere of the day became fresh and clean. In the plain it was enclosed and sultry still. But with the dark came the scents and sounds that make the world seem cooler and quieter. The group round the body moved, wrapped it in some sort of shroud, lifted it and began to take it away. No one tried to prevent them.

Though they had waited for the darkness, this was no surreptitious stealing of the dead hero's corpse. Torches and tapers were lit. A procession formed. Prayers were said. Some of those present carried cloths, stiff and stained with blood. These would become relics of great power and holiness. There was almost the air of a classical triumph: the conqueror had come home. Joy was more obvious than sorrow or, perhaps, the sorrow was of such an unusual kind as to be easily mistaken for joy or pride. One of the men there described his feelings:

> Between joy in his suffering and sorrow at still being here [myself], my mind is torn apart in different directions and twin desires overload a heart too small for them. Shall I sorrow that I was not his companion [in death]? But I must still triumph in his victory. Shall I triumph in his victory? I still grieve that I was not his companion. . . . That had been my intention. I revel in his glory much, and more than much. Still more I sorrow that I have remained behind.[1]

The processional lights wound across the plain and up to the city. This was the man who had made his Christian congregation significant, had raised it from obscurity to being one of the most important in the western world. He had had to contend with hatred from outside and bitter personal spite from within the flock. He had had to deal with deep divisions in the local church and in the church at large. He had had the wisdom and the love to surmount them. He had resisted the most powerful opponents and had had the courage to do unpopular things. He had rebuked the foolishness of the saintly as well as the wickedness of the proud. He had been lonely and yet able to love. He had known the discipline and the cost of love. He had known what it was to be misunderstood, accused of every kind of fault. He had been proud, sensitive, quick-tempered, yet had schooled himself into tact and diplomacy. When the Christian church in North Africa had been in desperate danger of destroying itself from within or of being destroyed from without he had saved it, largely because his own courage never wavered. He had given his spiritual children a new self-respect. And now they were bringing him home.

Just outside the gate of the city the great aqueduct, striding across the plain, came to the end of its journey and poured its water into the storage cisterns. Here the procession ended its journey also. There was a piece of open ground, named after a former procurator and used as a cemetery. The lights halted. The procession became a cluster. The liturgy came to an end. They buried the body and, still unmolested, went back to their homes. The man had been brought for the last time to his city.

Any uninvolved bystander who knew all these facts would be puzzled. The man who was being buried had begun his career as a martinet who appeared to take refuge in rigidity because he doubted his own ability to judge imaginatively. He had become the focus and centre of Christian imagination in Africa. He had failed in the first test but become the ideal of the Christian martyr. He had been the centre of every kind of divisive controversy and become the advocate of unity. He had been rejected by a large part of his flock and yet become the most powerful Christian leader in that part of the world.

The story of Cyprian's life is the story of how the cold disciplinarian became the hero of Christian Carthage.

2

As soon as one says or writes the word 'Carthage' one is caught up in a world of myth and counter-myth. A generation or two ago most schoolboys would have had a confused recollection of Hannibal and his elephants crossing the Alps, Cato's recurrent peroration 'Carthage must be destroyed', Dido's tragic farewell to Aeneas, and the great Marius, a fugitive, sitting on the ruins of the Punic city. Nowadays these episodes are probably less frequently remembered. But the wars between Rome and Carthage for the mastery of the Mediterranean are still part of a generally, if vaguely, known outline of the history of European civilization. Carthage, like Babylon, Athens, Jerusalem and Rome, has the romantic aura that attaches to the great cities of history. Travellers, scholars and journalists, have described what it is like to arrive there. Victorians came by steamer and wrote graphically of the feelings they experienced as they saw the famous coastline for the first time. Heroes of modern thrillers watch the blue-grey mountains of Tunisia solidify on the horizon as they peer from the windows of jet airliners. The romance is still there, and with the romance the mythology.

One of the much debated myths concerns Carthage as the 'gateway to Africa' from Europe. The geographical configuration has led scholars to argue that, so far from being an entry into Africa, Carthage is better understood as part of the ring of land round the Mediterranean and as having closer links with Europe on the northern shore than with the continent of Africa to the south. Nowadays Tunisia possesses a mixture of French and Arabic cultures and, in a sense, there is nothing particularly new about this. Long before Islam swept from east to west along the African coastline or nineteenth-century French armies began occupying Tunisian territory, both Near Eastern and Latin-European influences had helped to make the Carthage which Cyprian knew.

It is true that the mountains and the desert do cut the Tunisian coastal plain off from the rest of Africa. It is true that, on the whole, the coast itself is inhospitable and natural ports are not easy to find. Therefore this part of Africa tends, and has tended, to focus itself on the few ports that do exist and so to belong to the Mediterranean world. This has been especially true in those centuries when movement by sea was easier than long journeys by land over roadless territory. Nevertheless there is a sense in which Tunisia is still very much a part of Africa. Africa is a continent, not a single country, and just as Spain or Russia or Scandinavia can be felt to be part of Europe (however individual), so Tunisia and Carthage bear some of the marks of African as well as European and Semitic life. Birds, animals and vegetation are often typically African. Other parts of Africa south of the Sahara have a so-called Mediterranean climate, and sometimes one could be at a loss to know whether one stood outside Carthage or Cape Town. Even some ideas and traditional practices seem to be evidence that Carthage belongs in Africa rather than Europe, and long before Carthage existed there was probably contact between the people of the coastal strip and those who lived below the Sahara.[1] The only fair thing to say is that Tunisia has almost always been an area where European, Near Eastern and African ways of life have met and mixed.

If one can speak at all of 'original' inhabitants, those of Tunisia were the fair-skinned Berbers, Numidians, Gaetani or Mauretanians, as they have been variously called. Linguistically and racially they seem to have been a single unit. Then, from about the eleventh century B.C., there began the Phoenician settlement along the coast. Utica and other trading centres were set up by Semitic peoples who were not concerned with conquering the interior or with establishing colonies except in the trading cities themselves. They did not, therefore, do very much to build up a Phoenician civilization among the Berbers,[2] though a certain amount of intermarriage took place[3] and the Phoenician religion seems to have influenced the beliefs of the people of North Africa as a whole.[4] At this stage one may assume a sort of two-decker structure of population: there were Phoenicians established in trading cities on the coast, and there were Berber nomads in the interior. Some contact, sometimes close contact, sometimes actual intermingling, took place, and the Berbers themselves had remoter contacts with other peoples to the south.

Carthage was founded as one of these trading cities in the middle of the ninth century B.C. It also possessed this two-decker structure as regards population. The Punic part of its population probably never exceeded a hundred thousand[5] but its culture influenced a large part of the North African world. Indeed it became the most powerful of the Phoenician outposts and eventually the centre of a new sphere of influence. It established its hegemony over most of the western Mediterranean and so came into conflict with the emerging power of the city of Rome. From 264 to 146 B.C. there was a long period of rivalry between the two states. Three 'Punic' wars had to be fought before the issue was finally settled.

A clash of interests in Sicily started the open conflict. The first phase of the war ended with both sides exhausted and the island in Roman hands. In the second phase Hannibal carried the war into Italy and for the city of Rome there followed a nightmare period when its apparently invincible enemy seemed to have the whole peninsula at his mercy. But Scipio, taking a leaf out of the great enemy's book, invaded Africa, conquered almost all the Punic territory and forced the Carthaginians to sue for peace.

The Romans do not seem to have known how to deal with Carthage. Imperial administration had not yet developed sufficiently for the defeated enemy to be effectively absorbed. Inherited hatred made a lasting alliance impossible. To clip the wings of Carthage merely made her citizens more bitter. Rome, in any case, still feared her old opponent. Another war, ending in unconditional surrender, was perhaps inevitable. When it came in 149 B.C. the *casus belli* was an attack by Carthaginians, sorely provoked, upon a Berber ally of Rome. A long-drawn-out siege of the city followed and, when the final victory was achieved, Carthage was destroyed.

The destruction was as complete as the techniques of the time allowed. The city was burnt. The buildings were demolished and levelled. The ground was sown with salt to make it infertile. Solemn curses were pronounced against anyone who should attempt to refound the city. Some of the inhabitants were sold as slaves. Others presumably dispersed to find some sort of home and occupation where they could.

But Carthage was too valuable a site to be left totally unexploited forever. The very natural advantages which had led the Phoenicians to establish their trading post there meant that the city would be re-established sooner or later. An attempt was made by Caius Gracchus some twenty years after the destruction of the city, but it came to nothing. Yet the site was probably never entirely abandoned. Both Berber and Punic individuals settled among the ruins and some of the old Carthaginian traditions survived.[6] No further official colonization took place for almost a century, until the city was formally refounded by Julius Caesar in 44 B.C. Veterans from the army were sent out as colonists and soon Carthage had become the capital of a Roman province of Africa.

Initially the general commanding the army in the province was also proconsul of Africa and Numidia, but after A.D. 37, in the reign of the emperor Caligula, the civil and military authorities were separated. Africa proper, round Carthage itself and stretching to the south, came to be governed by a proconsul nominated by the Senate. He resided in Carthage and held office for a year. Numidia, to the west, was ruled by a legate whose appointment was approved by the emperor on the nomination of the Senate and was for an indefinite period. This official was responsible for the defence and military security of both provinces.[7] An important part of this military system was provided by the colonies of veterans who, in return for benefits and privileges, were expected to be ready to serve with the army in times of emergency.

There was thus added a third element to the already mixed population of Africa, a Latin and Roman element. But this time there was a real effort made to mingle the new settlers with the older inhabitants. One gets the impression that the *Punic*

Carthaginians tended to disappear as a class. Much of their culture and religion, even echoes of their language, survived in the province, but Carthage was essentially a Roman city. Whatever the racial characteristics of the inhabitants, whatever mixture of peoples they represented, their outlook and civilization was Roman. In other towns, especially those of military importance, the veteran colonists probably formed an upper or privileged class, with other inhabitants gradually acquiring more and more of the rights of citizens.

In the more rural areas—though not, of course, in them alone—were the Berber or Numidian people. Amongst them also some elements of Punic culture and some Punic blood survived, and there was no absolute, hard and fast division between town and countryside. When, therefore, in the later Roman empire, one finds the Christian religion making most headway in the Roman towns and cities and a great cleavage in outlook appearing between Roman-urban and Numidian-rural elements in the population,[8] one must not forget that there were also bridges between the two.

For one thing 'Roman' cities, though modelled on Italian prototypes with forum, baths, amphitheatre and all the status symbols of civilization, were not inhabited by citizens of exclusively Roman racial origin.[9] When they are described as Roman or Latin, the description is to be understood as referring to culture rather than to race. Racially the citizens of Carthage were probably as much Punic as Latin. It is hardly possible that there was no Berber element among them and, since Carthage was one of the great sea ports of the Mediterranean, it probably contained little groups of immigrants from all over the Roman world.

In the surrounding countryside also the racial distinctions would be blurred. In this case the merging was between Punic and Berber stock.[10] Moreover there were the great country estates, the 'villas', where the rich and important landowners with their employees represented an intermediate kind of life between the Roman towns and the Numidian countryside.

The divisions, both cultural and racial, were undoubtedly there. They were blurred and softened, one shaded into another; but they existed. The big towns were on or near the coast which curved to the south and east. As one went further into the interior, south and west, one moved away from the Roman sphere of influence. Settlements were smaller, villages rather than towns. Life became more primitive and rural, less Roman.

In the first half of the third century there was something of a civic boom in the province. There was much wealth for the ornamentation of towns and cities. There was an element of ostentation about African municipal affairs. One has the impression that a great deal of money and energy was expended to make sure that each city possessed, as far as was possible and on the scale that was possible, all the distinctive features of the metropolis itself. There is a common form of provincial civic pride, of course. British colonies in their heyday were littered with statuary, churches, town halls and railway stations modelled on English prototypes. Streets and hotels were named after metropolitan examples. Roman Africa was rather like that. Expatriate nostalgia, provincial determination not to be outdone, fashion and a simple desire to follow the best models would all play their part in this self-conscious Roman-ness.

There was a good deal of this even in Carthage. The city was wealthy. It was proud of being 'sister' to Rome itself, perhaps second only to the metropolis in the prosperity and the variety of its society. Carthage had its technologists and its artists, its famous lawyers and rhetoricians. But, as in Rome itself, dreadful poverty, widespread and appalling, existed side by side with the wealth of individuals and of the city as a whole. Again and again in Cyprian's letters there are remarks which suggest that the needs of the Carthaginian poor were like a bottomless pit into which charity could be poured endlessly without making very much difference.

The city itself stood on a headland that was shaped like a face in profile, with a huge nose and a straggly beard. Surrounded by sea and stagnant lagoon (which was the cause of regular epidemics of disease in the summer months), it looked across the great bay to other headlands and mountains opposite. The deep blue of the Mediterranean, the blaze of colour from the flowers, the rich look of the earth itself make a magnificent setting. But sometimes the countryside is a little disappointing, especially in the heat of summer when the dusty appearance of the thorn trees and aloes and the general dryness detract from its beauty. The coastal strip itself, on which the city stood, is fairly high, with cliffs rising from the sea, and hills behind them. But just a little inland the country is low and flat for some distance before the mountain peaks cut off the view. The climate is often hot, humid and sticky, though Carthage itself, being open to the sea, is not intolerable. In general there is an impression of abundant, vigorous life of all kinds, held in check a little by the heat itself, but always ready to burst out again when conditions are favourable.

The city was dominated by the Byrsa, which had been the citadel of Punic Carthage, and in Roman times held most of the great public buildings and temples, as well as private houses, some of them large and belonging to the wealthy. Between this hill and the port ran the main thoroughfares of the city, though most of the streets were narrow and overshadowed by very tall houses, which would tend to hold in the heat. Some of the wider streets were planted with trees to form avenues and many of the better buildings were built of or faced with marble. Large public baths and gymnasia, the circus and the theatre, and the tremendous aqueduct which brought water across the plain to the city, were all evidence of the progress and status of Carthage. The port was busy, and frequent contact with Rome and the rest of the world was possible. Grain and olive oil went out from the harbour to the imperial capital and contributed to the general wealth of merchant and landowner.

Beyond the city proper were the great gardens which were a Carthaginian tradition. Gardening was one of the few creative arts that had flourished in the old Phoenician days, and the garden suburbs were very beautiful. Populous, wealthy, pleasure-loving, seat of proconsular government and provincial officialdom, trading centre and seaport, Carthage was almost as important in the mid-third century as in her pre-Roman heyday.

There were only four ways out of Carthage. One was by sea. A road went north-west to Utica. Another went along the lagoon and then divided, one branch going westward and eventually reaching the coast again, the other striking south towards the inland frontier. Carthage was, therefore, both a natural centre or concourse and yet, at the same time, self-centred and self-contained. The life of the province poured into it. It was a place of exuberant, if slightly decadent, vitality.

A hundred years before Cyprian's time this city voted a public statue in honour of a man called Apuleius. He, like Cyprian, was an orator. His style was robust and vigorous, 'seasoned with piquant romance, horror, marvels and humour, and the whole was presented in a manner calculated to beguile the most jaded ear'.[11] His stories are bawdy, rumbustious and picaresque. He mirrors a world which was bursting with life and which was not terribly concerned with narrow morality. His *Golden Ass* is still readable and still read. All the lush vitality of Roman Africa is reflected in its tales, for all that it is set in a much more cosmopolitan world.

Apuleius was born in Numidia. After a chequered career and much travelling, he came back to Carthage. Carthage honoured him when his reputation was already made, recognizing in him something of itself. His reply pays the orator's homage to provincial pride, describing Carthage as 'so illustrious a city that it were an honour to her that a philospher should beg to be thus rewarded. . . .'[12] When, in his *Confessions,* St Augustine later described the city as a cauldron where illicit loves leapt and boiled,[13] he was probably thinking of the same exuberance, but seeing it through the sensitive, remorseful eyes of a convert. There is no reason to suppose that the spirit of Carthage had changed very much between the second and the fourth centuries, though her wealth and fortunes had fluctuated. Cyprian's Carthage, in the third century, would have the same flavour, boiling with vitality as well as immorality.

It would be a mistake to think that because the Punic city had been obliterated as far as possible, there was no real continuity between Roman Carthage and her remoter past. The histories of the Punic wars and the great scars which these had left on Roman memory, would be part of the heritage of 'Roman' citizens of Carthage. They might find themselves in an ambiguous position. Their pride as 'Romans' would identify them with the victors and not with perfidious Carthage, enshrined in Roman history as the home of treachery, lies and dishonour. But they would know also that their soil had produced Hannibal, perhaps the greatest enemy Rome had ever had to fight. Moreover, Virgil's tale of Dido and Aeneas had helped to weld the two Carthages together. Long before the Punic wars, the story said, there had been bonds between the Roman and the Punic nations. And in that story the perfidy was Aeneas's rather than Dido's.

The destruction of Carthage had not been followed by any attempt on the part of the Romans to root out Carthaginian culture. They seem, indeed, to have adopted at first a policy which made its survival inevitable. They presented the contents of the libraries of Carthage to their Numidian allies. The language of Carthage became the official language of all North Africa. It is true that the colonization under Julius Caesar modified this policy. A hybrid culture began to emerge. Carthage became more 'Roman', but there can be no doubt that the traditions of the ancient Punic civilization continued to live.[14]

Some of these survivals were obvious and everyday. The Semitic names which had been given to Carthaginian children continued to be given to other generations long after Carthage became 'Roman'. Latinized forms of these were even conferred upon African Christians, though their original significance had been derived from the beliefs and customs of Punic religion. 'The Carthaginian name system survived for a long time, and the African Christians who later invented such monstrosities as Quodvultdeus and Deogratias were still observing its essential rules.'[15]

Tertullian, who was the first great Christian writer of Africa and whom Cyprian regarded as his 'Master', was able to take it for granted that his readers would know these things. One of the arguments he uses would only carry conviction if third-century North African 'Romans' were familiar with the legends about the Punic Wars.[16] Since what he was writing was a defence of Christianity aimed at non-Christians, we may assume that this kind of knowledge was general. Roman Africa, as a whole, knew a good deal about its own ancient history and among Christians it was also remembered.

It has been suggested that the very character of Punic religion made North Africa a fertile ground for the spread of Christianity.[17] Conversion would deliver one from its harsh terror but would at the same time allow one to harness the rigorous enthusiasm which it bred. Christians would hear the story that crucifixion—the way in which the Lord died—had been invented in Carthage. They would feel themselves to be in contact with the roots of their faith, for they were in day-to-day contact with the vestiges of a religion which, because it was Semitic and Phoenician, was almost identical with the pagan idolatry attacked in the Old Testament.

When Elijah challenged the prophets of Baal on Horeb he was fighting against the very religion that had been practised in

Punic Carthage and had survived into Roman times. When African Christians heard the Old Testament denunciations of Palestinian pagans who sacrificed their first-born, they were hearing of precisely the same religion which the Carthaginians had practised, giving their babies as offerings to Baal. The very name 'Baal', which symbolizes idolatry, paganism and apostasy through much of the Old Testament, was still in use in third-century Africa. Those things in the Old Testament that seem most remote and unreal to twentieth-century Christians would have been vivid and close at hand to a member of the church in Carthage in Cyprian's day.

Carthaginian religion seems dark and cruel to the modern reader. It seemed equally so to the Roman authorities, and to the church, in the third century. The great national cult of Africa at the time was the worship of Saturn and Caelestis.[18] These Roman names scarcely hid the identities of Baal-Hammon and Tanit, the ancient deities of Punic times. It is probably impossible now to disentangle the origins of the cult and show just how these gods are related to the gods of Tyre itself from whose religion the Carthaginian beliefs derived. But it seems likely that both Berber and Phoenician beliefs contributed to the cult and that Baal-Hammon acquired the characteristics of several deities. He is certainly not the Roman Saturn. Perhaps the identification of the two was made possible because of the story that Saturn (the Greek Kronos) swallowed his own children. Certainly Baal-Hammon, like many of the Phoenician gods, received hundreds of infant sacrifices, as the rows and rows of tiny caskets uncovered in Carthage demonstrate. It is not surprising that he was regarded as a terrifying, implacable tyrant. His religion was a religion of fear. His worship had to be conducted precisely and meticulously. He had to be given his due. His will must be obeyed without question.[19]

The female divinity of North Africa was Tanit, who was also probably of Berber-Punic origin. In time she became even more important than Baal-Hammon. This may have been the result of a political and social upheaval[20] but the cause is unimportant. The goddess undoubtedly came to be regarded as the great mother of all things who was also, in a sense, the virgin queen of heaven, thus identifiable as Caelestis.[21] She also received her share of slaughtered babies.

In the second and third centuries the cult of Baal and Tanit, under the names of Saturn and Caelestis, became the national religion. The official Roman religious observances had their place, but the heart of the people was really given to the ancient gods of Carthage. This is not to say that Roman influences had no part in religious ideas. In the vast variety of cult and belief absorbed into the empire, the only course open to the authorities was the vigorous encouragement of syncretism and the approximation of one god and cult with another. A state completely neutral in religion was as yet unthinkable. The Roman pantheon, or its more elaborate and lively Greek equivalent, must be identified as far as possible with the national gods of the conquered peoples. Individuals, including Herodotus, attempted similar identifications either to amuse themselves or because they had incorrigibly tidy minds. There was inevitably some confusion. The personalities, characteristics and interests of the gods became somewhat blurred. There was some formalization, and a Romanized provincial no doubt thought of his gods very differently from his rural and simpler fellow-countrymen.

The amalgamation of deities in North Africa made it possible for Baal and Tanit, as Saturn and Caelestis, to exist happily side by side with the ordinary pantheon. But the effect of the process seems to have been that the old cult became more formal and more anthropomorphic. Whereas it had been focused on sacred places, groves and hills, and had possessed no buildings other than small shrines, Carthaginian temples of Saturn and Caelestis now began to be built on the more usual classical pattern. Earlier figures of the gods had been rough or symbolic representations of ideas. Later statues and pictures showed them in much more finished human form. But, since the bulk of the worshippers of Baal and Tanit were drawn from the countryfolk and the poorer classes in the town[22] it is probable that, beneath the late and formal attempts to make the cult respectable and to house it in conventional temples, much of the old practice survived.

There were aspects of the cult which Rome was compelled actively to discourage. Barbaric fantasies had to be disciplined and purged of those features which Romans regarded as immoral. Human sacrifice was forbidden, and Africans themselves seem to have turned away from it, substituting some kind of vicarious offering in its place in normal cultic practices.[23] But human sacrifice survived, at least on occasion, well into the Christian period. In spite of persuasion or compulsion, Punic ideas of the need to give the god one's own life, fully and directly, continued. Tertullian knew that human sacrifices continued to be offered in the Africa of his time. It was something that was still within living memory.[24] In Cyprian's day men and women thrown to the beasts in the arena were dressed as priests of Baal or priestesses of Caelestis.[25] In this way practices which the law permitted could be made to serve the old idea that the perfect sacrifice was one in which the offerer, in this case the priest himself, gave his own life.

Apuleius bears witness to a similar attempt to use a condemned criminal, not simply to provide a spectacle but to give verisimilitude to something else. In his *Golden Ass* the hero, while transformed into a donkey, is required to have intercourse on a public stage with a murderess who was subsequently to be eaten publicly by a lion. All this was part of the play.

> After this, a soldier ran along the main aisle and out of the theatre to fetch the murderess who, though condemned (as I have already explained) to be eaten by wild beasts, was destined first to become my glorious bride. Our marriage bed, inlaid with fine Indian tortoiseshell, was already in position, and provided with a luxurious feather mattress and an embroidered Chinese coverlet. I was not only appalled at the disgraceful part that I was expected to play: I was in terror of death. It occurred to me that when she and I were locked in what was supposed to be a passionate embrace and the wild beast, whose part in the drama would be to eat her, came bounding into our bridal cage, I could not count on the creature's being so naturally sagacious, or so well trained, or so abstemious, as to tear her to pieces as she cuddled close to me, but leave me alone.[26]

Apuleius exaggerates, no doubt, but the exaggeration would have no point if it were wildly beyond all bounds of possibility. The theatre and amphitheatre were homes of cruelty and vice and it is no wonder that Christians hated them. In Carthage the inherited cruelty of traditional religion gave them an added horror.

It is clear, then, that there was much of the old Punic Carthage, particularly in matters of religion, which had lived on through the destruction of the city, the rebuilding of a new provincial capital and the Romanization of Africa. Christians of the region knew that they were combating a paganism which went back to roots very like those of the idolatry of Canaan. Augustine recognized that the Punic language was not unlike Hebrew.[27] The law of Carthaginian priests, and even their name (*Kohanim*) was an echo of that of the Levitical priesthood.[28] Carthaginian magistrates bore a title derived from the same linguistic root as that of the judges of the Old Testament. An educated Roman Carthaginian of the third century could not but know his city's history and, knowing it, see all round him vestiges of an ancient Semitic heritage. If he were also a Christian, he would inevitably feel that much of this historic paganism had already been condemned, in clear, specific terms, in page after page of the Old Testament.

But it may be that there was something ambivalent in the North African Christians' attitude to the old religion. It has been suggested that, in spite of the official denunciations of paganism, some of the ancient attitude to religion survived among Christians themselves.[29] The element of terror and awe, which could degenerate easily into observance of religious laws from fear of eternal punishment; the tradition of rigorism and fanaticism; the eulogy of martyrdom and the belief that one ought to give oneself in death if one's faith was to be perfected; all these things can be shown to be parallel to features of the old cult of Baal and Tanit. It is possible that an attitude of mind remained constant in spite of changes in the form of religion. But this is not something which can, in the nature of things, be susceptible of proof. Nor must one fall too easily into superficial generalizations about African Christianity. A certain proportion of supposed converts in any given place and period will be superficial in their adherence to a new religion. Some (perhaps many) North African Christians would carry over to their new faith many of the psychological attitudes formed in them while they were devotees of Baal and Tanit. Not every Christian would do this. The more educated, more self-conscious and self-critical converts would be less likely to do so than those who were not used to examining their own thoughts and actions carefully. But even among the simpler people there would surely be many for whom conversion meant, as in a more modern Africa, freedom from fear and legalism.

At all events the known history of Christianity in North
Africa begins with martyrdom. Twelve men and women from
Scillium in Numidia were executed as Christians in the year A.D.
180. This is the earliest evidence we have for the existence of the
church in Africa. Attempts to reconstruct the rest of the story of
the origins of Christianity there are based on guesswork.[30]
Twenty-three years after the deaths of the martyrs of Scillium,
Perpetua and her companions were also put to death for the
faith. The tortures inflicted on them were of the cruellest kind
and the glory of martyrdom seems to have been greatly
enhanced in the popular view by the courage and faithfulness of
this small group of Christians.

By this time the church had gained the adherence of
Tertullian, perhaps the greatest African Christian writer before
Augustine. He had been born in Carthage about the year A.D.
160 and was at first a critic of Christianity and scoffed at its
beliefs. But he was converted, perhaps in Rome, at the age of
about thirty-five, and on his return to Carthage became a
leading figure in the church there.[31]

Always a rigorist, Tertullian set his face against any kind of
compromise with worldly standards. It is true that he allowed
some forgiveness of sins after baptism and did not completely
side with those, even more extreme, who regarded baptism as
one's final opportunity for repentance. He wrote, '. . . Although
the gate of forgiveness has been shut and fastened with the bar
of baptism, [God] has permitted some means of access. In the
vestibule he has stationed the second repentance to open to such
as knock: but now once for all, because now for the second
time; but never more, because the last time it had been in
vain.'[32] But when Callistus, bishop of Rome, allowed restoration
to repentant sinners who had committed gross and notorious
sins, Tertullian was appalled at the debasing of the purity of the
church which he believed to be implicit in such laxness. Any
kind of contact with paganism seemed to him a form of
apostasy which no Christian ought to tolerate. Again and again
he stressed the need for a strict asceticism so that Christians
would be toughened to withstand the test of torture and
martyrdom. To die for Christ was, in his view, the chief end of
man.

He was a prolific writer, and though we cannot be quite sure
which of his works belong to the earlier and which to the later

periods of his life, there is a consistent strain of strictness which runs through them all. He wrote on heathenism and idolatry, and in defence of the Christian faith. He wrote also on doctrine and on heresy, but most of all on asceticism. His work on the 'Soldier's Crown' shows how almost fanatical his rigorism could be.

By the time he wrote this treatise Tertullian had become a Montanist. This movement had begun elsewhere and had shown marked apocalyptic and pentecostalist features. But in North Africa it was chiefly noted for the strictness of its moral discipline and its insistence that there must be no attempt to escape from martyrdom. All these things made Montanism extremely attractive to Tertullian and it was in a spirit of disgust and impatience at the worldliness and temporizing of the official church that he proclaimed his new allegiance. Ironically, after a lifetime of sincere devotion to the ideals of martyrdom, Tertullian seems to have died peacefully at the age of sixty.

By this time the Christian church in Carthage had become relatively large, and we begin to know something of its organization and officers. Tertullian himself could speak of the growth of the church in his day. The names of some of the bishops of Carthage have come down to us. Early in the third century a council of about seventy North African bishops met in the city; Agrippinus, bishop of Carthage, was president of the assembly. The Carthaginian church was, by the middle of the third century, beginning to emerge from obscurity and to become the natural centre of Christianity in North Africa. This was the church to which Cyprian gave his allegiance.

3

WE do not know when Cyprian was born. It is usually thought that it must have been about the year A.D. 200, on the assumption that he was a man of some maturity when he was elected bishop in 248. We do not know whether he was actually born in Carthage, nor the history of the family from which he came. His background was that of an educated, well-to-do man, familiar with public affairs, and it has been said that he was of senatorial rank.[1] But we really have very little to go on except guesswork.

The chief reason for this gap in our knowledge is that the deacon Pontius, who wrote the first biographical memoir of Cyprian, chose to begin with his conversion to Christianity rather than with his birth. This, in turn, is usually attributed to the fact that the early Christians were more interested in eternal than natural life, and we know that Cyprian tried to cut himself free from his pagan past altogether, refusing even to quote from non-Christian literature. An admiring young clergyman—for Pontius clearly hero-worshipped Cyprian—might well believe that he was doing what his hero would have wanted. 'The actions of a man of God', says Pontius, 'ought not to be counted from any point other than when he was born of God.'[2]

It is, of course, possible that Pontius simply did not know

anything about Cyprian's life before his conversion. For what it is worth, Pontius seems to deny this. He hints that he could say a good deal about Cyprian's education and secular career if he wished to do so. One has to remember how short Cyprian's life as a Christian was. If Pontius was old enough to be Cyprian's deacon in 257, he was almost certainly old enough to be able to remember something about what he was like eleven years earlier. He could, at any rate, have found out a great deal if he had really wished to do so. There would have been many still living who would have remembered the days of Cyprian's conversion.

The other possibility is that Pontius deliberately distorts the picture. One can argue that he is so anxious to say only what is superlative about his master that he has left out everything else. In a sense this is precisely what Pontius claims that he is doing. He wishes to write a eulogy of a man of God. He can heighten the impression by omitting any reference to Cyprian's worldly achievements. But this does not necessarily mean that Pontius was inaccurate or unreliable in what he does say.[3] The probability is that Pontius' picture of Cyprian is based on Cyprian's own account of himself, reflecting Cyprian's standards of judging what was important and what was not. Obviously such an account will not be an objective one, but it will not necessarily be unreliable.

Pontius is open and frank about his main purpose in writing. During his lifetime Cyprian had been compared unfavourably with many of the heroes and confessors of the persecutions. Pontius wishes to show that he was at least as holy, as worthy of honour, as great in his sufferings, as any of them.

> It would, indeed, be hard if the passion of such a great bishop [*sacerdos*] and martyr as Cyprian were to be passed over, when our elders have so honoured laymen and catechumens who have obtained martyrdom. . . .[4]

This rather naïve piece of episcopal veneration gives us the clue to Pontius's whole approach. Cyprian's secular achievements would be inappropriate to his purpose because they might detract from the picture of episcopal dignity, holy asceticism and sufferings nobly borne which is what he is really concerned to paint.

One paragraph of a letter written by Cyprian after his

baptism may, however, reveal a good deal about his earlier life. The letter is addressed to Donatus, a friend who was, like Cyprian, a rhetorician and a convert. Cyprian says that he had always wondered how one could give up lavish banquets to become abstemious, gold and purple robes for simple dress, the emblems of office and civic honours for ordinary citizenship, crowds of clients and attendants for solitude.[5] He had learnt that conversion and baptism make every sort of renunciation possible. It is more than possible that one is being given a glimpse here of Cyprian's own pagan life.

We do know that Cyprian was thoroughly trained in rhetoric and was a teacher of rhetoric in his turn. This would have meant a wide literary education and an acquaintance with the great classics. It would also have meant that he had considerable debating skill and some experience as a lawyer or politician, and probably an administrative ability also. Wit, elegance and polish in written and spoken language, a clear logical mind in argument, and a graceful manner and appearance were the marks of the great orator, and in this period Africa was a hive of litigation and a training ground for legal pleaders. To make one's mark in these circles was to have a sure place in society, a popular reputation and considerable wealth.[6]

The orator's style was self-consciously elaborate, concerned with originality in expression rather than in thought. Brilliant imagery, convoluted, rhythmic sentences, exaggerations of all kinds from archaisms to newly coined and almost slang terms, were all woven together in the rhetorical style. The striving for the most striking, most captivating way of saying something which was not in itself particularly new was the principal pursuit of its practitioners.

Cyprian was also to acquire the reputation of having been an ardent supporter of what Christians regarded as devil-worship. Augustine, Jerome and Prudentius all have versions of this story. These men, contemporaries of each other, were born about a century after Cyprian's martyrdom and their testimony is not, therefore, of very great value. Nor are they entirely agreed on just what Cyprian was supposed to have done. Augustine says that Cyprian had devoted his orator's skill to preaching the doctrines of demons.[7] Jerome describes him as a champion of idolatry.[8] Prudentius accuses him of having been steeped in the black arts.[9] Just what this means is difficult to assess. Since Cyprian also acquired the reputation of having been a Christian wonder-worker and magus,[10] the fourth-century evidence may mean no more than that there was a vague memory in the church at large that Cyprian had had certain supposedly occult powers. Cyprian himself never refers to these matters directly. Even when he describes what he regarded as his vicious and meaningless life before conversion, with all the convert's and orator's exaggeration, there is no mention of either pagan priestcraft or magic.

There is in existence a treatise called *Quod Idola* or *De Idolorum Vanitate* which may or may not be by Cyprian. If it is his work, then it is a very early one and consists in large part of material derived from Tertullian or from another early writer called Minucius Felix. If it is not Cyprian's then it very early became associated with his name. In either case it is probably evidence of the traditional North African Christian attitude to pagan beliefs and suggests that Cyprian held to that traditional attitude.

De Idolorum, while it maintains that idols are empty and vain in the sense of being misleading, does not at any point imply that there is no spiritual power behind them. It is true that they are not gods, but the forces of evil make use of them to ruin the foolish. Demonic spirits operate the paraphernalia of pagan religion in order to dupe their devotees. If these religious observances do not appear to work, that is simply further proof of the deceptions which these devils practise.[11] So demonic powers haunt the idols and account for the prophetic frenzies of pagan priests, the answers given by oracle and lot, the shape of entrails and the flights of birds upon which the soothsayers base their predictions.

It is highly likely, then, that a man like Cyprian would believe that the pagan gods were real spiritual beings, even if they were not gods. If this was his attitude after he became a Christian then *a fortiori* he believed in their reality and power in his pagan days. The tradition that he was a champion of idols and a magus may contain an element of truth. He was neither a sceptic nor a mere formal performer of pagan rites. He believed in and relied on the power of the gods.

A belief in the reality of demonic powers seems to have been widespread in Africa. Cyprian certainly always believed in a real, literal and vivid hell,[12] and *De Idolorum* reflects the common view that Christ's and the Christian's power over the forces of evil is the proof that the one true God is the Lord of all things.[13] It would seem that the trump card in African Christian apologetic depended for its effect upon a real and widespread terror of the powers of darkness, now and in the hereafter. The talisman, the amulet and the magical sign to protect people from evil seem to have been in common use, and not only in Africa.[14] Black magic seems to have been widely practised. Apuleius has many references to it and was actually accused in the law courts of practising it himself. The very thin and feeble character of the evidence brought against him[15] is, by implication, evidence for popular willingness to believe in its reality.

This sense of a vast and powerful demonic world lying in wait for the unwary now, and able to hold him captive for all eternity, is important for understanding many of the things Cyprian says about the Christian church. When he talks of it as a place of certainty and security, when he stresses its sanctity and its role as the sphere in which the Holy Spirit operates, when he draws sharp distinctions between the true church and the false deluding sects, he is seeing it primarily as the fortress of the power of God within which one may be safe from this appalling destructive power of evil.

Apuleius once wrote a vivid and not entirely serious description of a magician at work. His contemporaries and Cyprian's would have accepted that description without question. Even if the magician was a figure of fun the powers which used her were not.

> When it grew dark, she climbed in a great state of excitement up to the cock-loft at the top of the house, which she finds a convenient place for practising her art in secret; it's open to all the four winds, with a particularly wide view of the eastern sky. She had everything ready there for her deadly rites: all sorts of aromatic incense, metal plaques engraved with secret signs, beaks and claws of ill-omened birds, various bits of corpse-flesh—in one place she had arranged the noses and fingers of crucified men, in another the nails that had been driven through their palms and ankles, with bits of flesh still sticking to them—also little bladders of life-blood saved from the men she had murdered and the skulls of criminals who had been thrown to the wild beasts in the amphitheatre. She

began to repeat certain charms over the still warm and quivering entrails of some animal or other, dipping them in turn into jars of spring-water, cow's milk, mountain honey and mead. Then she plaited the hair I had given her, tied it into peculiar knots and threw it with a great deal of incense on her charcoal fire. The power of this charm is irresistible —backed, you must understand, by the blind violence of the gods who have been invoked: the smell of the hair smoking and crackling on the fire compels its owner to come to the place from which he is being summoned.[16]

Cyprian, therefore, lived in a world where demonic forces, evil spirits and magic were real things, to be combated by every means possible. We need not suppose that, even in his pagan days, he was a practitioner of black magic nor that he indulged in the practices Apuleius was accused of. But plainly these things were not meaningless for him. Before he was a Christian he had put his faith in the gods to protect him from evil. In this sense he was 'a champion of idols'. After he became a Christian he put his trust in the power of the Lord of all things. As a bishop he would perform exorcisms and would regard them as a direct and immediate confrontation between the two powers. As a pagan he may equally have performed similar ceremonies to avert disaster, which modern man would describe as magical. Perhaps it was in this sense that he was 'steeped in the art of magic'.

Again, Cyprian like most of his contemporaries believed in the significance of dreams. In the Roman world dreams were counted as portentous, in the strict sense.[17] Apuleius too makes much mention of them and, perhaps they were given an even greater importance in his native Africa than elsewhere. Dreams were recognized as one of the most obvious and direct ways in which the gods communicated with men. Even the command to become a Christian could be conveyed in this way.[18] Throughout his life Cyprian attached great importance to dreams, allowing himself to be guided by them and regarding them as portents and prophecies of what was to come. This trait in his character has been recognized so often as not to need labouring again. But what is significant is that even his contemporaries were apparently a little shocked by his attitude.[19] One is forced to conclude that, in this matter too,

Cyprian's attitude was more than mere convention. He really believed that the divine will was manifested to him by dreams, and this may have an important bearing upon what he said about inspiration.

For anyone who knows the modern continent of Africa this matter has a particular interest. African traditional religion has laid much stress upon dreams as a vehicle for making known the divine will or, more often, the wishes of the ancestors. Christians also attach much significance to dreams and it is known that a clergyman may trace his sense of vocation back to a dream, on occasion a dream in which (non-Christian) ancestors have indicated that he ought to become a Christian or be ordained.[20] There are close parallels here with the attitude of many Christians in Cyprian's day. This is not to say that there is some direct historical connection between the religious beliefs of Roman North Africa in the third century and Bantu Southern Africa in the twentieth. Nor would one wish to resurrect the once popular hypothesis that all African religion had a common source. It is simply that direct personal experience[21] of those who regard dreams as a divine mandate makes it easier to understand Cyprian. It becomes perfectly credible that Cyprian should combine what some would regard as 'a superstitious faith'[22] with great practical ability and a hardheaded grasp of administrative detail.

Cyprian's decision to become a Christian seems to have been the result of a disgust with the world in which he lived. He wrote about the apparent decay of the world to one of his friends. The winter brings too little rain; the summer is not as hot as it used to be; even the mineral deposits are not as easily worked as in the past. Men leave the land; soldiers and sailors cannot be recruited; there is no honesty in business and no justice in the law. Art and morals are both declining. Cruelty and lust are regarded as entertaining. The smell of death is everywhere and yet, apparently, no one stops to remember the warning of his own mortality.[23]

We are very familiar with this sort of reaction. Everyone remembers his own childhood as bright with incredible summers. Presumably this is because while he is growing, his excitement at discovery and expansion projects itself on to things around him. When he is older, when vitality is waning, greyness seems to predominate, and this also is projected on to empire which drew its members from all groups and classes and yet managed to weld them into a single whole.[27] As the community grew in size it naturally became more difficult to maintain that unity. Perhaps the congregation could no longer be fitted into one building. At any rate a special place for worship would be needed.[28]

Very little is known about church building before the fourth century. What little evidence there is suggests that the only thing which distinguished a building used for worship from a private house was pictures or other decorations, and this presumably explains why so very few churches can be identified by archaeologists. They existed, but they were no different from other houses. This would fit in entirely with what we know about some Jewish synagogues, which were attached to or actually within private houses.[29] Sites exist where it seems possible to trace the precise architectural development. A house, a simple church and then a more elaborate building succeed one another on the same piece of ground.[30] As the congregation grew larger a house with a single spacious hall would have to be used, or else several rooms would have to be thrown together. Early churches retained the many-roomed character of private houses built round a courtyard, and there are examples of this type of building in North Africa.[31] Moreover there were large rooms or basilicas (not to be confused with the royal basilicas which provided the almost universal pattern for church building after the third century) in many private houses belonging to wealthy citizens.[32] We know from Tertullian that there were special buildings used for worship half a century before Cyprian's day,[33] and we shall be fairly safe in conjecturing, considering the rapid growth in the size of the congregation and the general trend of the time, that throughout Cyprian's life as a Christian the church at Carthage met either in the basilica of some private house, or in a house which had been converted for the purpose by the demolition of interior walls.[34] The bishop or some of his clergy may well have lived in the house, as seems to have been Jewish practice.

Cyprian would therefore find himself attached to a sizeable and growing community, just beginning to find its home and focus in a definite building. It would have outgrown the older stage of simply meeting in any convenient room. It would probably not yet have begun to design and build special churches; it was in the stage between. It had a permanent and recognized meeting place, but one which was, perhaps, a little makeshift, adapted from other uses. The sense of having no abiding city in this world would still be present. At the same time the community was expanding—a waxing, crescent society, so to speak—experiencing new life and growth. It was precisely the situation likely to appeal to a man who had come to realize that pagan Roman Africa was dying.

This community possessed in its clergy a recognized body of officials who were probably, like its buildings, in an intermediate stage. They were developing from an earlier, informal, 'part-time' ministry, but not yet quite so highly organized as they were to become in the fourth century. This was the period when what could be called an embryo parochial system was beginning to emerge. In Rome the clergy were being allotted districts for which they were responsible,[35] and in Carthage the same sort of thing was happening.[36] All the evidence suggests that the clergy had become a full-time ministry, paid for their work and no longer needing to support themselves by secular employment. They had become the *ordo* as opposed to the lay *plebs*.[37] Presumably their numbers were also tending to grow as the size of the church increased, and the fact that they were beginning to be assigned to particular districts suggests that the Christian community no longer formed a single congregation.

One of the clergy, Caecilius, was largely instrumental in Cyprian's conversion.[38] Presumably it was Caecilius who was given the job of instructing the new catechumen, but such a deep friendship grew up between the two that Cyprian actually took the other man's name and, on Caecilius' death, was asked to look after his wife and family. It would be nice to be able to say that the widow and her children provided the celibate Cyprian with a ready-made family but, in fact, they disappear from the story probably to become simply a part of the much larger family for which the future bishop would have to assume responsibility. The direct care of and provision for a great number of dependants, who would otherwise be destitute, was still a most important (perhaps the most important) part of the church's pastoral work.

Cyprian's decision to remain celibate and forgo sex, marriage and family was taken before his actual baptism.[39] It was part of his self-imposed discipline and his determination to the majority of new converts. It would seem that some of the old rigorous attitudes of the African church were no longer so vigorously maintained. The very fact that this was a period in which numbers were increasing fairly rapidly suggests that there were likely to be relaxations of standards. Certainly the intense shame which Cyprian later expressed at the falling away of Christians at the first onset of persecution suggests that this was so. The less rigorous attitudes seem to have been adopted by the converts drawn from the wealthier classes. [45] If this was so then Cyprian was not only isolated from the majority of Christians by his social standing, but also, by his rigid moral outlook, from those relatively few converts who shared his intellectual and social background.

There is, in fact, a certain ambivalence detectable in Cyprian's attitude to contemporary society. His letter to Demetrianus suggests, as we have seen, that in one sense Cyprian hankered after a dignified, moral Roman past and that he became a Christian, at least in part, in revulsion against the degradation of Roman society. He longed for the kind of world that there had once been. This was a common attitude of the time. Even the very phrases Cyprian uses can be paralleled from many contemporary writings.[46] What was unusual about Cyprian was that he sought to find what he longed for within Christianity. Others who sought the same things more usually believed that Christianity was undermining the old Roman virtues.

It was, of course, true that Christianity did reject most of the values of even the most conservative Romans. Tertullian stood for the tradition that the Christian ought to have nothing to do with the culture, thought, comforts and status symbols of pagan society.[47] We know that Cyprian, too, believed that being a Christian meant abandoning the outward trappings of wealth and success, and the style and apparatus of pagan learning. His disgust with a world which had abandoned its old values had brought him to a position of even more radical rejection. It was a hard and lonely position, one in which a certain appearance of puritanical rigidity is not surprising.[48] 'A catechumen must not sin,' he wrote[49] and he deliberately divested himself of anything that was the least bit likely to lead him into temptation.

Cyprian was probably baptized at Easter in the year 246. In the glory of the North African spring, with its promise of a new cycle of life, he was exorcized to cast out the powers of evil, he renounced the world, the flesh and the devil, the sinful past was washed off in the font, and he emerged clean, white-robed to take his place in the redeemed eucharistic community. Everything in his character and background conspired to make the impact of the rite particularly powerful. No doubt what he wrote to Donatus is coloured by the fact that he was a new convert, full of the enthusiasm typical of a convert. No doubt the tricks of exaggeration proper to a rhetorician were more difficult to put off than worldliness and fornication. What Cyprian actually said was,

> But after the stain of earlier years had been washed away with the help of the water of new birth; and a light from above, serene and pure, had been poured into my forgiven heart; after a second birth had remade me a new man by means of the spirit breathed from heaven; then in a wonderful way what had been doubtful became sure, what had been hidden was revealed, what had been dark was lit up, what had seemed difficult before could now be attempted, what had been thought impossible was now able to be done . . .[50]

It is the account of a man who takes seriously a commitment to a personal revolution. Everything belonging to the old life has to be abandoned; the new life must be lived without compromise. Not only is this revolution real, in the sense that Cyprian's renunciation is practical and uncompromising, it is also real in the sense that he finds himself able to meet the demands made upon him. The vivid symbolic structure of the baptismal rite was quite literally made a practical reality in Cyprian's everyday life.

The same revolution of renunciation and new life can be seen in Cyprian's writings. In his first few months as a Christian he produced the *Testimonies,* a three-volume collection of scriptural texts, two dealing with the great events of salvation and the third being more concerned with the life, morals and faith of the Christian.

The existence of the *Testimonies* raises all the problems connected with the North African Latin bible. No one can be quite certain precisely when it came into existence, or exactly what it was like. The fact that the account of the death of the to wonder whether he meant something more than this—a dream, perhaps—or whether he literally expected some providential intervention to prevent the choice falling on the wrong candidate. An ecstatic utterance by a recognized prophet within the congregation might have served, for prophets were still known in North African Christianity in this period.[3] Whatever the particular form the judgment took, Cyprian was clear that God had chosen him and was, therefore, confident that he could do the job in spite of the fact that he was still a novice. Such confidence is not always attractive.

Others were, in any event, not so confident of him. It was inevitable that there should be some jealousy on the part of those who had been Christians and presbyters far longer than he had. But some of the best and most sensible men also seem to have had their doubts about Cyprian. Pontius tells us that some of those most opposed to his election were later won over by Cyprian's wisdom and moderation and by his refusal to bear a grudge. This argues that they had been moved by genuine doubts about the rightness of the choice and not by personal spite. They were evidently fair-minded enough to admit their mistake. They were also later amongst Cyprian's closest friends which, in turn, argues that they had the qualities he could admire; so not all the opposition was captious. But some of the bitterest of the dissidents were moved by nothing more than furious resentment.

From the very start Novatus emerges as the figure round whom the opposition gathered. Novatus's duties as a presbyter were in the district of the Byrsa, the citadel of the ancient Punic city. Standing on a hill overlooking the sea and containing the Praetorium and the Forum, the great temples of Juno and Aesculapius, and the Platea Nova, one of the few wide streets of the city, this would have been one of the most important 'parishes' in Carthage. Novatus was therefore eminent among the clergy. We only know him through Cyprian's eyes and Cyprian was not above trying to stir up popular feeling among the laity against Novatus.[4] He appears as a senior man in both years and experience, but easily bored by routine and already rather suspect. He and four other presbyters were always the core of the opposition and they were joined later by a deacon called Felicissimus, who was to be a tower of strength to them.

But Cyprian appears to have been accepted, and presumably

consecrated, by the other African bishops, for he always insisted that he had been elected with their consent. This must have strengthened his position, but his life cannot have been an easy one when five of his clergy were openly and vehemently opposed to him, particularly when those five may have represented between one fifth and one tenth of the higher orders.[5] They made it clear that they would welcome an opportunity to disobey his instructions.

Cyprian's greatest weakness lay in the fact that he was so new to it all, not only to the episcopate but to the church itself. It was not simply that his newness caused jealousy, but that he had had so little experience upon which to base his judgment. He had to take over the reigns of government in the church without having had the benefit of watching his predecessors in office over a long period. He had to familiarize himself with a bishop's duties, perhaps on the basis of formal and definite rules as to what he should do.[6] He had to exercise this brand-new authority in the face of a restless and dissident group within the congregation. The eighteen months of peace which the new bishop enjoyed before the persecutions started were spent chiefly in administration. If he appears to have behaved, during this time, with the opinionated inflexibility of a very new broom, that was only to be expected. Upon his conversion to Christianity he had reacted with puritanical severity. He had needed time to come to trust his own judgment and develop his own ideas about the faith. His elevation to the episcopate seems to have had the same sort of effect. The very weakness of his position drove him to behave with an appearance of authority and decisiveness.

He had first to win over those whom he could from the party of his opponents. He seems to have had a fair degree of success, but the hard core of opposition remained. One cannot imagine that he found this easy to bear. His watchword was 'discipline'[7] in those early years. The church must be trained in all its ranks, like an army, so as to be what Cyprian believed it was. Having turned away from a dying pagan world, he was horrified to find some of the same failures within the church itself. He corrected them with firmness. He did not stifle his real feelings in order to charm his enemies. His ability would convince those who were genuine and sincere in their opposition that he was able, after all, to assume his new duties. He appeared very sure of himself.

have survived. But there is enough evidence in the writings of Tertullian and of Cyprian himself for us to be able to reconstruct fairly fully the form which the service probably took.[15]

It is just possible that the eucharist was celebrated every day, but the great eucharist was on Sundays and the bishop was, of course, the celebrant. The service began with the lections from the scriptures, read by the inferior clergy, while the bishop sat on his special chair made of wood and covered with a linen cloth. A raised dais in the middle of the congregation would give Cyprian the slight eminence needed to make himself seen and heard while he preached the sermon that followed. He would normally sit to do this (like all teachers in the classical world of the time) and his style would presumably be smooth and polished as befitted a trained rhetorician. No doubt what he said would also be full of clear and firm demands, like his letters, and studded with quotations from scripture. Then, with the congregation facing east, there followed the prayers of the faithful, which were perhaps quite literally 'common' prayers in which anyone could join.[16] At this point either Cyprian's chair would be moved back to the end of the church where the presbyters sat, or a table might be placed in front of him.[17]

The offerings of bread and wine were brought up by the faithful and from them Cyprian took sufficient to communicate the congregation. By this date this phase of the service had become a great ceremonial act, a peak point for the congregation in which they participated fully and actively. Cyprian is also, so far as we know, the first person who regularly uses the term 'sacrifice' to describe the eucharist.[18] How far the development of the offertory and the growth in the use of sacrificial language went together we do not know, but it is clear that Cyprian was thinking of far more than simply the people's offering of bread and wine for use in the sacrament. His language is so forceful and direct that it is possible that he was thinking of the eucharist as being a direct parallel with pagan sacrifice. God's favour is strictly limited to his worshippers who have something to offer that is acceptable to him, in this case the passion of Christ.[19] If this really is what Cyprian believed it would reinforce his theology of the church as sharply demarcated from the secular world, where the power of evil was unchecked, and equally sharply demarcated from false heretical sects, where the true power of God was not to be found.

Having taken bread and wine, the bishop then mixed a little water with the wine in the cup. Here certainly the action represented, for Cyprian, something much vaster than would appear on the surface. It symbolized in microcosm what the whole rite achieved: the union of the people of God with the Lord Christ.[20]

Then, with his flock round him, Cyprian would summon them to lift their hearts to God. In the prayer of consecration he was probably still largely free to follow his own wishes as to the actual words and not yet bound to a single set form. But he would end by calling his people, again, to join him, using the prayer of Christ himself, 'Our Father . . .'. Then came the kiss of peace, symbolizing the love which bound together the Christian family. And then Cyprian gave each of his children a piece of the consecrated bread while his deacons administered the cup.

Here, at least, the church was what it was meant to be. It was compacted in a defined unity in Christ. It was laying aside the memory of the old humanity and the former worldly way of life and, therefore, was released from the torment of remorse for sin by the joy of God's forgiveness.[21]

But the world was not going to allow the church, or Cyprian, much peace. The emperor Philip is said to have been favourably disposed towards Christianity or, at least, to have wished it no harm. In 249 there was trouble among some of the legions stationed in the Balkans. Philip sent a senator, an elderly man called Decius, to restore order. The mutiny ended in the legions declaring Decius their emperor. Decius marched against Philip, who was defeated and killed in mid-249 and was succeeded by his opponent.

It would seem that Decius' attitude to the pagan Roman world was, in a great many ways, very like that of Cyprian. He was quite as much disgusted by the decaying moral standards and the degenerate society of his day. But his reaction was different. Like so many of his predecessors he believed that a return to the traditions of classical Roman life would provide a solution. He failed to perceive that a moral outlook and climate cannot be induced artificially by edict. He did not, like Cyprian, turn his back on a dying society and immerse himself in a new and growing one; he tried to force society itself back into an earlier mould. Roman ideals, Roman manners and customs and Roman religion were to be restored in their former shape.

It is not, perhaps, surprising that Decius should have decided that the Christian church, which differed from him so radically in its belief about the proper cure for the world's diseases, should be compelled to abandon that belief. The persecution began within six months of the new emperor's accession. While some of the earliest persecutions had been local, sporadic and the result of popular disturbance, the third-century attacks upon the church tended to be official, sustained, widespread and systematic efforts directed by the central government. It is true that there had not been many of these. The church, on the whole, had been left in peace for a good many years before Cyprian's election as bishop, and this fact may partly account for the increase in the number of adherents. But the later persecutions had shown a disturbing development. The government was learning more about Christianity and more about the most effective ways of dealing with it.

Decius' programme shows every sign of his having learnt from the mistakes and achievements of earlier persecutors. By the beginning of 250 the government had initiated its campaign for the destruction of the Christian church. So far as possible local authorities were left no alternative but to carry out their orders ruthlessly. A date was fixed by which time the inhabitants of each province of the empire were to make a public declaration of their allegiance to the gods by sacrificing, dressed in the traditional robes of pagan ritual, at a temple specified by the authorities. Written certificates were issued to prove that the act had been performed. The net was extremely fine-meshed, for it seems that the people of country villages and estates, as well as the larger towns, were compelled to answer the roll and perform their religious duty.[22]

In Carthage a large number of Christians did not wait to be called. All Cyprian's insistence on discipline could not prevent their flocking to the Byrsa to perform the rites required by Decius' edict. They did not wait to be arrested and questioned but climbed up the hill themselves, running to the market place as if, Cyprian said, they could not wait to embrace eternal death. The magistrates could not always cope with the crowds whose terror made them demand to be allowed to apostasize at once. Mothers carried or dragged their children to the ritual. There was a terrible, panic-stricken rush to make oneself safe with the government.[23]

Or, at least, this was how Cyprian remembered it—as a degradation of the whole church. He seems to have felt that it was a very definite personal disgrace for the bishop, too. Everything he had tried to do and all the principles for which he had stood were just swept away in an insane anxiety to be physically safe. The other memory which remained with him from these awful weeks was the mindless, blood-lustful shouting of the crowds in the city streets, 'Cyprian for the lions'.[24] For Cyprian, who had a particular horror of the arena, its cruelty and the dehumanizing effect of its spectacles,[25] this would have been the final degradation.

The imperial edict had appointed five commissioners to act with the local magistrates to secure the apostasy of as many Christians as possible, and that of the bishop in particular. At first, it seems, the officials were not entirely ruthless, but the arrival of the proconsul in Carthage in April 250 put an end to any leniency. Torture was used for the first time and some of those who had managed to hold out against the earlier pressures now gave way. There were many hundreds of acts of apostasy. There were also many instances of great courage. Since the purpose of the government was to break the courage of the Christians rather than to kill them, there were many who survived in spite of the cruelties they had passed through. When the proconsul left the city to tour the province and increase the tempo of the persecution in other towns and districts, the church in Carthage was in a tragic condition. Some Christians had died. But this was not the real problem. It was the survivors who, by their very existence, caused the crisis. Some had survived by their resolute courage and faith, in spite of punishment and torture. Others had survived by cowardice and apostasy. The church was torn apart by something far worse than a mere quarrel about who should be bishop.

Cyprian himself left the city early in the year. The proconsul had not yet arrived and the persecution had not, therefore, reached its highest pitch. Before the real crisis came, Cyprian had withdrawn to comparative safety. This is an action which is very difficult to understand or explain. He may simply have been unable to face the thought of martyrdom. His horror of the arena was very real. But if this was the case he behaved very cleverly afterwards. He consistently refused to justify or excuse his conduct. He never behaved as public figures usually behave,

just as Cyprian took refuge elsewhere. It is difficult to imagine
how otherwise he would find spare bishops, conveniently to
hand, just when he needed them.

Cyprian found no peace and quiet in his hiding placeeeee.
Besides the press of practical business he was a desperately
worried man. He was in a state of continual anxiety about the
flock he had left behind. He was worried about what would
happen to the large numbers of very poor Christians who
depended on the bishop's charity.[37] He was worried about the
confessors in prison and the agonizing penalties inflicted on
them.[38] He was worried that the clergy might fail in their duties,
or might (alternatively) be over-zealous and do something silly,
and draw the attention of the authorities to themselves.[39] He
was deeply shamed and depressed by the mass apostasy. He
was probably uneasy about his own withdrawal. Above all he
was acutely aware of the divisions that existed in the
Carthaginian church, and he believed that these weakened the
church not just physically but spiritually.

The bishop seems to have been particularly disturbed by
dreams and visions at this time. One imagines that they were a
symptom of the tremendous inner turmoil of a man caught up in
a frightful dilemma, as well as of his fears and anxieties for the
future of the church. He dreamed that a voice said, 'Ask, and it
shall be given you.' In his dream he was evidently present at a
gathering of the local congregation for the voice went on to
direct the people present to pray for certain persons by name.
But the church was not united in prayer for there were dissident
and conflicting voices. This angered the Lord who desired the
harmony and unity of his people. Cyprian significantly
concluded from this vision that it was disobedience to Christ's
command to love one another which had brought these
sufferings upon the Christians of Carthage.[40] Christ had
promised to grant the prayers of those who agreed on earth.
Since there was not perfect love and agreement in Carthage,
Christ could not be expected to grant their petitions. Cyprian
wrote to his people, urging them to pray for deliverance and
faith.[41]

Not all his dreams were so pessimistic. He also believed that
God had told him that peace was coming and that the trial
would go on only a little while longer to test those who stood
firm. But he warns his people that only prayer and fasting will

enable them to retain their faith and courage.[42] There were very good grounds for his anxiety. The sharp contrast, already referred to, between those who survived by courage (the confessors) and those who survived by cowardice (the lapsed) could not but lead to all sorts of unhappiness.

In the early stages of the persecution the confessors seem to have behaved not only with exemplary courage but with a breadth of charity appropriate in Christ's saints. They were ready to forgive the fallen. This aspect of the confessors' activities has not really received the sort of recognition that it ought to be given. It would have been so easy for them to have adopted a holier-than-thou attitude and to have demanded that the lapsed be excluded from the church forever. Such a reaction is what one would have expected in the rigorist traditions of the African church. But there seems also to have been a tradition that the confessors could pardon, or at least procure the pardon of, the lapsed. This the Carthaginian confessors now attempted to do.

At the same time the popular veneration for the confessors reached new heights. They were treated almost as if they were already martyrs. Even Cyprian is constant in his praise of them. His letters contain frequent references to their courage coupled with exhortations to further steadfastness. Again, he shows no sign of guilt, no fear that his own behaviour might be unfavourably compared with theirs. And, as with the virgins, he insists that self-sacrifice is not to be an excuse for other kinds of un-christian behaviour. The very fact that confessors are heroes of the faith means that they must be heroic also in such things as humility and obedience.[43] The danger of the situation lay precisely in the fact that the confessors could so easily be tempted to pride. They seem to have avoided the worst and most obvious kind of pride, the rigorist and puritanical kind. But in their anxiety to be charitable, flattered by popular veneration, the confessors fell into a more subtle temptation. They began to claim the right to restore the lapsed to full membership of the church. With Novatus waiting for the chance to assert himself against Cyprian, with Cyprian relatively new to his office, somewhat discredited, and away from the centre of things, a critical situation rapidly developed.

the persecution to allow the restoration of the lapsed. His reply, then as ever, was that he was not willing to take action on his own. When he returned, a corporate decision could be taken.[21] At that stage, perhaps, both Cyprian and his opponents were acting honestly and with the best of motives. A little willingness to see the other point of view might have prevented the schism. Now, joined by an unnamed fifth presbyter, the dissident clergy had the opportunity to take the lead in a widespread popular movement. The confessors' action in pardoning the lapsed swamped the church with those whom they claimed to have forgiven.[22] This, in itself, meant that the party of the Five Presbyters gained enormously in strength and popularity. Cyprian was in the invidious position of having to insist that the heroic confessors were destroying the true church and that those who rejoiced in being restored were merely building one sin upon another. His reaction to the false position in which he felt that he had been placed was a savage one. He accused the Five Presbyters of deriving the same sort of pleasure from the church's disarray as the dirty old men derived from Susannah's shame.[23] The reference is, of course, to the story of Susannah and the Elders in the Apocrypha. Since the point of that story is the acuteness of Daniel in detecting a false accusation its applicability is not immediately apparent, unless it lies in the play upon the word 'elder' (presbyter). But it does show the strength of Cyprian's resentment.

Nevertheless the Five continued to restore those who could claim, in some degree or another, to be the recipients of the confessors' clemency. The more they readmitted, the greater their popularity and the support they received. The vast numbers involved and the change of attitude on the part of the confessors had destroyed the African tradition of rigorism. Cyprian, the runaway, now appeared to be the champion of what had become the unpopular cause.

This was, as we have seen, hardly Cyprian's true position. He had already begun to move away from the very strict viewpoint of Tertullian. He had, in effect, been defeated in every single attempt he had made to devise a policy to deal with the situation and minimize its divisiveness. He had been put in a false position and he had been reduced in the end to one delaying tactic: the attempt to persuade everyone to wait till the end of the persecution should come. Perhaps the one thing he had discovered was precisely that the old rigidity would not provide the answer.

Cyprian's opponents received further encouragement when they were joined by the deacon Felicissimus. He was already a man of considerable reputation and he became so eminent that Cyprian began regularly to refer to the dissidents as 'the party of Felicissimus'. One of the advantages that Felicissimus possessed was that he controlled considerable sums of money (whether officially as a deacon or in his own right) which he used for the relief of the poor, or at least for the relief of those poor who supported him. On the surface this could be made to look like bribery and Cyprian made much use of it as propaganda. But he also, in several of his letters, directed that his own funds should be used for the needy and one can hardly suppose that he intended this to include the supporters of the other party. It was six of one and half a dozen of the other.

It may be that almsgiving had a particular significance for Cyprian over and above issues of charity and party support. In his treatise *De Opere et Eleemosynis* he had maintained that good works such as almsgiving could atone directly for sins committed after baptism. The treatise was almost certainly written early in Cyprian's life as a Christian bishop[24] and its argument is part and parcel of his cut-and-dried (and unattractive) theology of church and ministry. The same sort of teaching appears also in his treatise on the Lord's Prayer where, again, he seems to be saying that a selfish motive for almsgiving is perfectly acceptable. Apart from his emphasis upon a Christian law and some of what he says about good works atoning for sin, it has to be admitted that Cyprian is on rather surer ground, however, in this part of his teaching than in some of the things he says about the priesthood. It is all very well to criticize him for teaching a selfish attitude to almsgiving, advocating that one should be generous in order to save one's own soul. But Cyprian believed that he was doing no more than apply passages like the parable of the sheep and goats. He would not be the only person to have drawn this conclusion from much that the New Testament says.[25]

Whether Cyprian was justified in taking New Testament promises of the blessings that follow from generosity as an argument to back up his point of view or not, it is clear that what he taught about almsgiving tied in very closely with what he taught about the ministry as the authorized agent for the dispensing of God's forgiveness. It may be that the function of ministers in receiving alms from the faithful and distributing them to the poor was, perhaps even unconsciously, a symbol of their wider authority. At any rate, there was Felicissimus, established in Novatus's 'parish' on the Byrsa, holding services, dispensing charity, announcing that Cyprian's followers would receive no alms and would be denied the sacrament even on their deathbeds, and, in general, behaving as if he were an alternative bishop in everything but name. The schism had become an open one.

Now Cyprian was forced to see that even his one consistent argument was not very convincing. He had maintained, over and over again, that everyone should wait till the persecution was over and the normal processes of discipline could be reinstated. Circumstances simply would not allow matters to wait like this. Genuinely penitent apostates might show a new courage, defy the authorities and die. The summer months brought epidemics. Simple old age carried off the lapsed like anyone else. It was not enough to say 'wait', for death would not wait and a Christian could not refuse forgiveness to the dying. This was the strength of the confessors' case and it was exploited to the full by Felicissimus and the Five. Cyprian himself became aware of the need to make allowances. Though he continued to maintain the necessity of reserving all normal cases till peace came, he had to concede that those in danger of death and in possession of a letter from a confessor might be given the sacrament after being restored to communion by the laying on of hands by one of the clergy. Those who lacked a confessor's commendation were not to be restored even if they were dying.[26]

Such a ruling was clear-cut and still harsh. It was, in fact, far too clear-cut even for the cases with which Cyprian had had to deal. There were so many varieties of people, all appealing for mercy, and any of them might find themselves in danger. There were those who had first sacrificed but later found new courage and were banished, losing their property. There were those who had been dragged by their relatives and friends to the place of sacrifice and physically forced to make the necessary gestures. There were those who had sacrificed to save their families. There were those who had never sacrificed at all, but had merely pretended to do so. Cyprian found that he lacked the sternness to apply his own clear-cut rules.

It was the last class of the lapsed which was to become the biggest problem of all. In a sense their existence was a consequence of the very way in which the persecution had been organized. If each city and province was to be visited and each person compelled to answer his name and perform the necessary rites, then there must be some record to show who had sacrificed. Therefore certificates (*libelli*) were issued. These consisted of a statement identifying the person performing the sacrifice and an endorsement witnessing that it had been performed.

The certificates that have survived[27] read like this:

> To the commission chosen to superintend the sacrifices at A; From XY, son of Z, of the village of A, aged so many years, with such and such distinguishing marks.
> I have always sacrificed to the gods and now, in your presence, in accordance with the edict, I have sacrificed, poured libations and tasted the offerings, together with the named members of my family.
> I request you to certify this below.
>
> I, B.C., witnessed the sacrifice of you (and your family).
>
> Date.

The form is sufficiently constant to suggest that it was standardized. We know that a vast number of them was issued because of the high percentage of Christians who acquired them.[28] The clause 'I have always sacrificed' need not be taken too seriously, for a Christian who was prepared to sacrifice at all would not boggle at stating that he had always done so. But it was not only the sacrificers (*sacrificati*) who acquired the certificates. One of the people about whom Celerinus wrote to Lucian was Candida, of whom he says that she gave presents in order not to sacrifice and simply went up to the Capitol and down again without performing the actual rite.[29] There were very many Christians who possessed certificates and who nevertheless asserted that they had not sacrificed.

Christians might have acquired such certificates in a variety of ways. There were, no doubt, some officers who offered false documents out of kindness, others in return for a 'gift'. But there seems to have been a tradition that if one made a statement in writing that one had always sacrificed to the gods and was willing to do so again, this would serve instead of the actual rite. And there is a suspicion that the authorities condoned the practice. This suspicion is strengthened by the large number of certificates issued in this way. After all, the government did not desire to make martyrs. The whole pattern of what was done tended in precisely the opposite direction. The great crime of the Christians was their resolute refusal to allow any form of syncretism. So it was important to break the corporate strength of the church and to force Christians to modify their intransigent monotheism.

Bishops were seized, and often executed. That was intelligible as an attempt to render the church leaderless. Other Christians caught in the fine-meshed net were banished, turned into displaced persons without privilege or status of citizenship; others were sent to the mines; others had their goods confiscated. Those who were arrested were tortured, frightfully ripped by an iron claw. Some of them died in the process, but clearly the purpose of torture is not to kill but to compel a man to do or say what the torturers want. The obdurate, having undergone the 'purple confession' of the claw, were left to die of thirst and starvation. Lucian, for all his pride and pomposity, wrote movingly to Celerinus:

> . . . We were ordered to be put to death by hunger and thirst and were shut up in two cells that so they might weaken us. . . . Moreover from the smoke of a fire our suffering also was so intolerable that no one could bear it.[30] But now we have reached radiance itself.

He sends greetings of peace to the lapsed in the name of the martyrs who

> were put to death in prison by hunger, whose companions you will hear us to be within a few days. For now there are eight days from when I was shut up again to the day on which I have written my letter to you.

Torn, starving, tormented by the acrid smoke, without even water to drink, Lucian felt that after a week of this treatment death was very near. But the point of such punishment was precisely that it was likely to procure apostasy. A man might

very easily deny Christ for the sake of a drink of water, and the
government would have won a notable victory.

It is plain, then, that all these punishments were designed not
to result in a martyr's death but to make it almost impossible for
a Christian to remain faithful. The availability of false
certificates could have been a psychologically more subtle but
just as effective means of compromising the members of the
church. Once accepted, such a certificate bound its holder to
some sort of acknowledgment of the gods and thus weakened
the church's exclusive claim to absolute loyalty. For the
ordinary Christian men and women of Carthage, not very
brave, perhaps only superficially converted to the new religion,
it would have seemed so easy. They knew the quite frightful
penalties of obduracy. They were offered an opportunity of
escape without actually committing the blasphemous action,
and they seized the opportunity in their hundreds.

Though these people, the certificated (libellatici), thought of
themselves as having avoided the ultimate sin of actual
apostasy, there was a sense in which what they had done was
worse than the action of the sacrificers. Cyprian solemnly
declared that they 'polluted their consciences by immoral
certificates in not the slightest degree less' than the sacrificers
contaminated their hands and mouths by the sacrilege of
offering and eating at the heathen altars.[31] This stern judgment
he was later to repeat, adding,

> Such a profession [of willingness to sacrifice] . . . is the
> solemn testimony of a Christian who disowns what he has
> been. He says that he has done exactly that same action that
> has actually been committed by another. It does not matter
> whether he has made public what he has done or had less
> disgrace or guilt among men. He will not, in any event, be
> able to escape or avoid God his judge. . . .[32]

For the certificated had, like the sacrificers, obeyed men rather
than God and they had added a lie to their willingness to disown
the faith.

There were, therefore, two kinds of certificates circulating
among the lapsed. The one was issued in the name of the
confessors and martyrs and claimed to grant, or at least pleaded
for, peace and forgiveness, making the recipient safe with God.
The other made him safe with the state. There was no reason

Five, if they had a place at all, were simply part of the clergy. They could no longer claim to exercise emergency authority in the bishop's absence. The broad popular support which the combined opposition had been able to draw upon was that very part of the church which was now no longer quite so certainly the church at all—the lapsed. If their cases were to be examined they could not be treated as members of the Christian assembly which would judge those cases. Now that the long-promised action was being taken at last, there was no longer the same urgent necessity for them to ask for special favours. It would be better to wait a little longer and be reinstated by unquestioned authority.[39]

All this, no doubt, explains why Cyprian so soon re-established himself in Carthage. His return itself caused the opposition to melt almost overnight simply because the aims of the various elements were no longer congruous. The opposition had lost the initiative. No doubt recognizing this, Novatus set off for Rome at about this time.

6

THE slackening of the persecution which allowed Cyprian to return home was not quite that great 'peace' for which everyone had been longing. But at least it was quiet enough for the demand for a settlement not to be deferred any longer. Things had become far easier for Cyprian, not only because the persecution was less fierce but also because the opposition within the church was so much less active. Yet the very policy he had been pursuing through all these difficult months now made its own demands.

Cyprian had argued, over and over again, that corporate action must be taken to solve the problem of the lapsed. He had said that this corporate action must involve the whole church: the whole church in Carthage, and the church in the whole world.[1] Probably at first this was not, and was not intended to be, a carefully thought out and theologically self-conscious definition of 'the whole church'. One of Cyprian's favourite arguments had been the neat but not particularly logical one that peace must come to the whole body before it could be given to the individual.[2] His immediate concern had been to preserve the rights of the bishop and the normal penitential discipline.[3] But in spite of his high view of his office, he was reluctant to act alone. From the very beginning of his episcopate he had said this repeatedly,[4] and for someone whose advancement had come so quickly and with so much controversy, it was surely both natural and wise. To argue, therefore, that common counsel must be taken was not only tactically sound but was also a matter of principle. The same reasons would commend to Cyprian the idea of a gathering of bishops. His correspondence with Valdonius and with the Roman clergy had strengthened his hand in moments of crisis, enabling him to say that he was acting in concert with the church elsewhere. It would again be good tactics to be able to say that the final policy was one on which many bishops had agreed. The problem was one which affected the church all over the world; a universal solution to it was highly desirable. Not for the last time Cyprian found that events dictated a particular course of action and that action, in turn, led to the development of new theological principles.

Once committed to common action, Cyprian was obliged to initiate it at the first possible moment. Councils of bishops had already met earlier in Africa, as elsewhere.[6] We do not know how regularly or how frequently they had met, nor how far they had become an institution. But plainly it would be sensible, natural and desirable (and sometimes really essential) for bishops to meet and decide on common policy. Constitutional and canonical authority was probably not thought out at that early date. Each bishop was a person of weight, and possessed authority in his own church. If they met together they could hope to arrive at a common mind. This could be expressed in a written document as the decision of the gathering. It would possess the moral authority of the collective assent of the bishops. Much of what Cyprian said later about the nature of the bishops as the bond of unity of the church is really quite simply giving expression to some *de facto* natural process such as this.

A council of bishops assembled at Carthage in the spring of 251. We know very little about them as individuals, what the size and extent of their sees was, or even how many bishops there were in Africa. More than a century later, when North African Christianity was split by the Donatist schism, much play was made with the tradition that a bishop must preside over a proper town or *civitas,* not over some rural community.[7] Moreover at this time Christianity was still overwhelmingly an urban religion. It is not till after Cyprian's time that it began to establish itself in the rural areas of North Africa. So it has to be assumed that the bishops who came to the council were heads of Christian communities in the towns. There were, of course, a considerable number of sizeable towns, and we do not know how many of them had Christian congregations. Nor do we know what proportion of the bishops actually came.

We do know that the organization of the church tended to follow the lines of civil authority. Therefore it would be natural for the African bishops to assemble in Carthage, the capital of the province, and for Cyprian to preside over them. It is highly unlikely that there were metropolitans in any strict sense as early as the middle of the third century, but his personal character, ability and education, his occupancy of the most important see and his own urgent need for decision, made Cyprian the obvious leader. At any rate, preside he did. A large number of others besides the bishops assembled in the church in Carthage. Cyprian speaks of his 'brothers' and 'the people', but presumably the clergy were present, too.[8] The council was obviously intended to fulfil both of Cyprian's promises: to consult the whole church in Carthage, and to act with his fellow bishops.

From the very start the members of the gathering were reminded that they were part of a larger Christian church than that of Carthage or even Africa. Just before the meetings started two letters arrived from Rome. One was the notification of Cornelius' election. The other was a bitter and vehement protest from Novatian, declaring that Corneliuus was not the true bishop.[9] Faced with such contradictory accounts of the Roman election, the council decided to send Caldonius and Fortunatus to investigate the whole matter. This action was perhaps not surprising, though it surprised Cornelius. The African bishops had met to patch up the divisions in the church. They could hardly act in concert with Cornelius if he was himself no more than the leader of a faction in Rome, especially as he represented the laxer one. There was the possibility that Cornelius might be the Roman equivalent of Novatus, and that Novatian, backed by the confessors, might be a sort of Cyprian, standing for righteousness and the traditional penitential discipline.

But there is just a hint that there was a little more to it than that. The African bishops had an opportunity to assert themselves. Caldonius was very much Cyprian's man. He and his colleague were told to find the bishops who had consecrated Cornelius, check on his credentials and obtain a written statement about the true facts. They were also to try to act as peace-makers. Until they reported back, none of the Africans would treat Cornelius as bishop of Rome. They would deal with the clergy as a body, as though the see were vacant. Cyprian was, perhaps, too human to be able to resist paying Rome back in its own coin. His conscience, at any rate, was rather tender on this point, for he felt it necessary to justify himself to Cornelius for refusing to recognize him immediately as bishop. A lengthy explanation of his actions was sent to Rome.

The council in Carthage had other matters to deal with. Novatus had gone, but Felicissimus was still about and he was, perhaps, the most important of the dissidents. Moreover, if Cornelius were to prove to be not only the rightful bishop of Rome but also, like Felicissimus, an advocate of easy restoration for the lapsed, the Carthaginian deacon might be able to justify his actions by reference to the Roman bishop's views. It was highly desirable, therefore, that the gathering should pronounce on the illegality of Felicissimus' policy as soon as possible. This it did, probably while Cyprian himself was away from Carthage. He was making sure that the decision not to deal with Cornelius direct was put into effect elsewhere in the province.[10]

Then two African bishops, Stephen and Pompey, who had been on a visit to Rome, returned and assured the council that Cornelius really was the rightful bishop.[11] Caldonius and Fortunatus had not yet arrived back, but there could be little doubt about the nature of the report they would bring. The council was compelled to recognize Cornelius and to lift its embargo on letters directly addressed to him.

The Roman opposition had not yet shot its bolt. Four more travellers crossed the Mediterranean and appeared at the council. They included a presbyter called Maximus and a deacon called Augendus, and they had come to announce the election and consecration of the new and rightful bishop of Rome. But their candidate was Novatian.

They were too late. The African bishops had satisfied themselves that Cornelius was the true bishop. The period of doubt and hesitation was over. Maximus and his colleagues were turned away from the assembly. Cyprian, who had been used to say that those of the lapsed who were not willing to wait for restoration could secure it by being crowned as martyrs,[12] found himself allied with Cornelius whose reputation was for extreme leniency. The fact that Cornelius' election had been so obviously genuine, the appalling bitterness and spite of Novatian's delegates, and their outrageous behaviour,[13] had compelled him to recognize that this was his brother Christian and fellow bishop.

Novatus, too, found himself with strange bed-fellows. He had left Carthage when Cyprian's return brought an end to his laxist policies. In Rome he had allied himself with Novatian and the confessors against Cornelius, taking the side of the rigorists. The explanation may lie in the different traditions of Rome and Africa. It may be that Novatus simply could not bear the authority of any bishop. It may be that he preferred to be on the side that had the support of the confessors, who had been laxists in Carthage and were rigorists in Rome. It may be that he simply could not resist the opportunity to intrigue. But, whatever the reason, Novatus's alliance with Novatian would bring Cyprian and Cornelius closer together. Cyprian very soon drew Cornelius's attention to the trouble caused at Carthage by Felicissimus and the Five Presbyters.[14] What had emerged quite clearly was that the unity of the church, within each city and between city and city, was not dependent upon complete agreement on the vexed question of the lapsed, but upon the relationship of the bishop to his own people and to other bishops. Cyprian and Cornelius came together not because they agreed on matters of doctrine and policy, but because each was the bishop chosen by his own church and recognized by neighbouring bishops. Novatus and Novatian each represented a vociferous minority which refused to accept the decision of the majority. As had happened before, the press of events was forcing Cyprian to accept new ideas.

In the midst of all this excitement it is something of a marvel that the council was able to concentrate on the matter of the lapsed at all. Cyprian delivered a long address on the subject to his colleagues. His *De Lapsis* reads like a rhetorician's allocution. He begins by thanking God for the restoration of peace. Then he turns to the confessors upon whom 'we look with joyful countenances'. 'You have resisted the world bravely.

You have given God a glorious spectacle. You have been an example to your brothers who are yet to come.'[15] This is their hour of triumph and let no one despise it.

He then, rather obviously, defends his own actions, arguing that those who did not deny, by implication confessed. Those who withdrew were also refusing to deny Christ. The confessors, no doubt, have the first place. The second goes to those who withdrew to cautious retirement and were, therefore, preserved for God! The greatest sorrow for the church is that she has lost so many of her best children by martyrdom.

Why, then, one might ask, did God allow the persecution? It was a test rather than a punishment, Cyprian replied—and one can imagine his voice growing sterner. The church had become too soft; wealth, greed and luxury undermined the primitive purity and morality. 'In the bishops there was no religious devotion. In the ministry there was no sound faith. In works there was no mercy. In morals there was no discipline.'[16] The terrible indictment went on, in language worthy of Tertullian. The church had been warned. Prophecies, visions, and scripture itself, had told Christians what to expect. And yet, before the persecution had really begun, the majority of them, knowing the eternal punishment for idolatry, had not so much fallen as jumped into sin.

They ran voluntarily to the forum; they rushed spontaneously to [eternal] death, as if this were a thing that they had yearned for beforehand, as if they were seizing an opportunity [now] given which they had always wanted.[17]

But to many their own destruction was not enough. Encouraging each other, the people were urged to ruination. They drank to each other's death in the fatal cup.[18]

There were those who excused themselves on the grounds that the tortures threatened were so awful that they could not stand against them. Such an excuse, said Cyprian, would be bound to earn sympathy. One could forgive those who had given way at first and then had gone back to face the torturers. One could forgive those who were too weak to withstand the agony of pain. 'But now what wounds can the defeated show?' Have they proof that they tried to withstand torture? Or did they give in because their faithlessness came even before the struggle began?

Perhaps Cyprian felt that he was over-doing the harshness of his strictures, because he then explained that a good doctor is compelled to be rough and to hurt his patients if he is to get to the bottom of the trouble. Gentle treatment is superficial and does not really do any good. But then Cyprian turns to the whole question of the movement led by Felicissimus and the Five. One gets the impression that this was what he really wanted to say. Nearly half his treatise is devoted to an attack upon those who had acted as if open and public discipline were not necessary for the readmission of the lapsed to the fellowship of the church. Inveighing against the breaking of the laws of the gospel, telling horrific stories of what had befallen those who tried to do so, reasserting the need for humility and obedience, Cyprian warmed to his theme. It was in the course of this restatement of the need for patient, deep and genuine repentance that he also dealt with the case of the certificated and the reality of their guilt.[19] His main concern was to show that forgiveness is not something to be won cheaply, and that the shepherds of the flock are damaging those whom they wish to help if they gloss over the horrors of apostasy.

No one present can have been left in any doubt about the views of the president.

I entreat each of you, beloved brethren, to confess his sin, while the sinner is still in this world, while his confession may be accepted, while the satisfaction and remission made by the bishops are acceptable to the Lord. Let us turn to the Lord with our whole mind and let us, expressing our repentance for our sin with real sorrow, entreat the mercy of God.[20]

Cyprian concluded what he had to say with a great call for real penitence.

[God] is able to give pardon, is able to set aside his judgement. He is able mercifully to forgive the penitent who works and prays; is able to look favourably on whatever is sought on behalf of such as these by the martyrs or done for them by the bishops. Or if anyone moves him more with his atoning deeds . . . he gives weapons again for the conquered to be armed with. . . . The soldier will seek his contest anew, will repeat the fight, will provoke the enemy, and by his very suffering will be made stronger for the battle. Who thus satisfies God; who, by penitence for his deeds, by shame for his crimes, has conceived more of both virtue and of faith from sorrow for his fall itself, having been heard and forgiven by the Lord, shall make that Church joyful which he had earlier saddened: and he will now not simply merit pardon from the Lord, but a [martyr's] crown.[21]

With this statement of the case before them, the bishops decided on the procedure to be adopted in dealing with the lapsed. Cyprian had nowhere actually said in so many words what he thought ought to be done, but the implications are clear. He had stressed the real horrors of sin, the need for genuine penitence, the pastoral foolishness of allowing the lapsed to return too easily. He had insisted that the certificated were as guilty as the sacrificers. He had reiterated the importance of maintaining the traditional discipline, public confession and public restoration. He had said, clearly and unequivocally, that it was God's priests, the bishops, who should handle the process of restoration, though recognizing the right of the martyrs to plead for the penitent.

Cyprian had thus emerged for the moment as the leader of the party which was really rigorist in its outlook. He was not prepared, as Tertullian had been, to limit the scope of God's mercy. Nor was he willing to insist that only the pure could truly be within the church. Yet he seems once again to have swung back to a more stern opinion. He will not say that the door of forgiveness is ever closed; he will not, on the other hand, allow sinners to be told that sin does not matter. Above all he insists upon authority, discipline and obedience and the orderly way of doing things. The other bishops were, perhaps, less stern. They agreed that each case should be examined on its merits and allowance made for the reasons why each of the lapsed had fallen. The certificated could be restored after a period of penitence and on the authority of the bishop. The sacrificers would be restored only after a lifetime of penitence. Those who had refused to admit their guilt were not even to be restored when they were in fear of death.

That Cyprian loyally accepted this decision appears from an interesting letter written to a fellow bishop, Antonianus, which is also our only source of information about the decision.[22] Antonianus had obviously been tempted to prefer the rigorist Novatian to Cornelius, whom rumour accused of being willing to communicate with the lapsed as Felicissimus's party had done. Cyprian's doubts and hesitations appear quite clearly in the letter and he often seems to be trying to convince himself, rather than Antonianus, that the decision has been the right one. But he defends Cornelius generously and is determined that a common mind and common action must be achieved. His devotion to authority and orderliness has triumphed over his rigorism. And, perhaps, he had begun to have doubts about the validity of a semi-rigorist position. He points out that, if one of the lapsed in fear of death is restored to the church and then recovers his health, a bishop cannot be expected to deliver the *coup de grâce*.[23] For there was this anomaly implicit in the bishops' decision. The situation would inevitably arise in which the healthy lapsed must wait indefinitely for forgiveness while others, who were no less guilty, might be restored in time of sickness and then recover to be full members of the church. They could neither be re-excommunicated nor killed, simply to tidy up the problem. But obviously the robust, patiently enduring perpetual penance, might feel some resentment. And after everything Cyprian had said about the iniquity of the certificated, the sacrificers might also complain at the severer treatment meted out to themselves.

One cannot help but wonder whether what was happening to Cyprian was not precisely parallel to what had happened when he became a Christian, and when he was first made a bishop. In each case he began by maintaining a very narrow and stern point of view; then the press of events made him modify his attitude in practice; then he developed a new theological principle to take account of the situation which he had come to understand more profoundly. Much the same pattern seems detectable here. Cyprian is again at the start of a new phase in his life. He is having to function for the first time as a bishop among bishops and as *primus inter pares,* at that. He begins by enunciating stern and unyielding moral principles. But he is also committed to the principle of common episcopal action and the consensus of the other bishops is less rigid than his own opinion. He is also sensitive to pastoral problems and begins to see that even the more lenient attitude of the majority of his colleagues is not pastorally feasible. So he moves, once more, into a gentler, more flexible, position.

To suggest that Cyprian was becoming hesitant and tentative would be quite ridiculous. Nothing could undermine the confidence and certainty which he always exhibited. But there does seem to be a new awareness and a willingness to be less absolute in his opinions. The touch of humour in his remark about a bishop delivering the *coup de grâce,* ponderous and macabre though it may be, is something new. It almost looks as if this was the turning point, after which Cyprian became a more sensitive, more mature person, willing to trust his own judgment rather than to rely simply on what he believed to be the inflexible standards of past generations. He had, after all, been through a harassing time. He had been compelled to reconsider his own earlier attitudes not only by the dissidents who had opposed his authority with such comparative success, but also by his colleagues and, in a sense, by his own behaviour. Moreover, the situation in Carthage was very different from what it had been when he had first become a bishop three or four years earlier. Then he was dealing with a community which had been left in peace for several years, which had just begun to draw in relatively large numbers of converts, and where the standards had been somewhat relaxed. Now he was pastorally responsible for a shattered church, almost broken by persecution, where the great need was for healing and reunion. It would not be surprising to find that the martinet of earlier years had been softened by his own experience and the tribulations of his people.

Cyprian had also become convinced that the solution of African problems could not be found in isolation. From this time on he became more and more involved with the church elsewhere. He had always been on good terms with the confessors in Rome. Now that the African bishops had given their support to Cornelius, Cyprian set himself to win the confessors away from Novatian. In this he was still very much the old Cyprian. His favourite technique had always been to try and discover the hidden differences within the opposing party, bring them to the surface and rely upon the logic of the situation to do its work. He wrote[24] to the confessors, with all the prestige of the man who had stood firm for discipline in Africa, urging them to place orderliness and unity before faction. Cornelius was soon able to send him a moving description of the reconciliation.[25] The confessors had submitted, recognizing Cornelius as the only rightful bishop in Rome and asking to be taken back into the fellowship of the church. The people were almost delirious with joy at the news. A spontaneous demonstration welcomed the confessors back into the congregation. Cornelius, true to the generous, forgiving policy he had always upheld, turned to Maximus, the leading confessor and a presbyter, and reinstalled him in his place amongst the clergy. It was, said Cyprian when he heard the news, as though the trophies of a great victory had been brought back to the place where they belonged.[26] It was also, he realized, a recognition of the fact that the church contained tares as well as wheat.[27] The Tertullianist and Novatianist puritanism simply was not a tenable position.

The church in Rome, like that in Africa, held an assembly to decide what was to be done with the lapsed. Novatian's rigorism was excluded. The laxity popularly attributed to Cornelius was also rejected. The final decision, as in Africa, was for a middle course, neither puritanical nor easy-going. Similar views were expressed, and decisions taken, in the east. It looked as though the whole church was slowly coming to a common mind which admitted that even the gravest sinner must not be finally excluded from the church without hope of forgiveness but, on the other hand, maintained that this forgiveness must not be too cheaply offered.

Novatus was still to be a problem for Cyprian. The defection of the confessors inevitably diminished the popular appeal of Novatian's party in Rome. Cyprian had supplied Cornelius with details of the unpleasanter episodes from Novatus's past.[28] It must have suited both schismatics to part company. At all events Novatus went back to Carthage,[29] accompanied by a deposed bishop called Evaristus, to see what could be done to advance his cause. But for the moment it was trouble from outside rather than from within which disturbed the church in Carthage most. In the last months of 251 Decius appointed to an office modelled on that of the censor, traditional guardian of ancient Roman morals, a man whose views on the proper cure for the ills of society were similar to his own. His name was Valerian and he was eventually to become emperor himself and continue the general policy of Decius.

But Decius' reign was nearly over. He was killed, together with his son, fighting on the Danube frontier against the Goths. The new emperor, Gallus, took over the government towards the end of 251 and managed to negotiate some sort of settlement with the Gothic invaders. But Africa was far from peaceful. There were savage reminders that civilization was precariously maintained against the barbarity of non-Romans and that, beneath the veneer of culture and progress, there were dirt and disease. In 252 Numidia was subjected to a raid by Berber tribesmen and large numbers of people, including some Christians, were taken captive. In the same year the plague struck at Carthage. It seems to have been part of a widespread and devastating epidemic. Some five thousand people died in the city of Rome each day, while the plague was at its height there. The Roman armies, and those of their enemies, were devastated by it. In the city of Alexandria half the population either died or fled.[30]

For Cyprian these tragedies had two chief consequences. First of all he was compelled to face the pastoral implications. From his earliest days as a Christian he had been particularly sensitive about the need to give away what he possessed to those who were less well off. Much of his correspondence in the days of his exile refers to charity and works of mercy. In Carthage the poor were certainly omnipresent and a bishop's job consisted largely of trying to meet their needs. The new tragedies were new challenges. Somehow Cyprian raised a very large sum of money, perhaps the equivalent of £1,500 or £2,000 in modern currency, which he sent to the bishops of Numidia to use in ransoming the captives taken in the Berber raid. His letter[31] is a little essay on the theology of interdependence, written round the theme 'if one member suffers, all the members suffer with it'. To his letter he attached a list of all those who had contributed, so that the Numidians could remember them in their prayers.

The plague was a much larger problem and it needed to be met with greater resources of both practical aid and theological acumen.

Everyone was trembling, running away, shunning contagion, disloyally putting their own friends out as if by excluding one person who was certain to die of the plague, one could exclude death itself. All over the city the carcases (no longer bodies) of many lay about in the meantime, forcing the passers-by to pity themselves by looking at what would happen to them in their turn. [But] no one thought of anything but his own cruel gain. No one trembled at being reminded of a like event [coming to himself]. No one did to another what he would like to happen to himself. . . . [Cyprian] first of all urged on the people assembled in one place the benefits of mercy. . . . Then he next added that there was nothing marvellous in looking after our own people alone. . . .[32]

So the money was found and the services provided to meet the needs of the sick and dying, whether Christian or not.

Again practice had to be backed by theory. This is the period in which Cyprian probably produced his treatise addressed to Demetrianus. In it he deals with the problem of disaster and suffering in contemporary society and attempts to explain why Christians are still subject to evil though they alone are servants and instruments of good. It is plain that the tragedies and disasters have raised doubts and difficulties for Christians. Prayer and love and caring for others are part of the answer to the existence of evil. But Christians cannot expect to find their life made easy in a world which is essentially rotten.

Indeed, the second consequence of the crises of 252 was the outbreak of further persecution. Sacrifices were ordered by Gallus throughout the empire, to avert the plague. Christians could not, of course, participate. For this they were subjected to new horrors, perhaps as an officially organized punishment, perhaps as popular revenge for their failure to help placate the gods. This new persecution seems to have lacked the systematic ferocity of Decius' campaign against the church. The threat of death was real enough, however, and there were many pathetic cases reported to Cyprian. If death were imminent, whether from plague or persecution, then a good case could be made out for a further relaxation of the regulations dealing with the lapsed. They could all be said to be, in a sense, in danger of death. Was it fair to expect them to continue faithfully to accept the church's discipline and refrain from communicating when they might be arrested at any time?[33]

We have already seen[34] how Cyprian, though instinctively

preferring a rigorist policy, could not at the same time bring himself to place limits on Christian forgiveness. He had also detected the flaw in the decision adopted at the council. Both logic and the pastoral demands of the situation required that an even gentler policy should be followed.

As usually happened when he was anxious and unhappy, Cyprian was tortured by dreams and visions. No doubt he was uneasy about the policy adopted; his conscience as a pastor was always acute and sensitive. He felt deeply for those caught between the cruelty of society and the discipline of the church. He believed that God was trying to warn him about the violence of the struggle that was coming and of the need to close the Christian ranks against it.

The African bishops met again, and this time they decided that those of the lapsed who had been consistently penitent, faithfully accepting the discipline imposed on them, should be restored to the full fellowship of the church. A solemn, formal document,[35] headed by the long list of the names of the bishops present, was sent to Cornelius in Rome to explain this change of policy. There is very little doubt that it was actually written by Cyprian himself. The style is his, or very like it. The arguments, as in his earlier letter to Antonianus, read as though he is really trying to convince himself that the bishops have done the right thing. He is deeply concerned to stress that the new leniency is not a matter of indulgence or of condoning the weakness of those who do not care. It is a matter of absolute necessity, a preparation for the battlefield for those who really have shown in every possible way that they are penitent. To refuse them peace would be pastorally negligent or cruelly harsh. Once he had said that the lapsed could always redeem themselves by seeking martyrdom. Now he specifically says that such an argument is a betrayal of pastoral trust. He has moved a very long way.

Inevitably Cyprian's final abandonment of the rigorist position meant that he was faced with two opposition parties instead of one. The rigorists, who sympathized with the Novatianists in Rome, felt that they had nothing further to gain from following Cyprian. The laxists rallied their forces to fight for an even easier treatment of the lapsed. Privatus, a bishop deprived of his office long before 'for many and grave crimes,'[36] seems to have thought that, if pardon was being granted more freely to sinners, he would ask for his own sentence to be reviewed. When this was refused by the council, Felicissimus seized the opportunity presented to him. After some scheming and a lot of careful publicity, one of the Five Presbyters (Fortunatus) was consecrated by Privatus as the rightful bishop of Carthage in place of the puritanical Cyprian. At much the same time Maximus, who had appeared at the first council of Carthage as Novatian's spokesman, was chosen by the Novatianists as the rightful bishop in place of the hopelessly lax Cyprian. What part Novatus, once Felicissimus' friend and one of the Five, subsequently a supporter of Novatian in Rome, played in all these plots and counter-plots is not clear.

Cyprian must have felt for a while that he was right back in a situation like that of the first outbreak of persecution under Decius. The church was divided, undermined from within, under fierce pressure from without. But, in fact, the persecution seems soon to have slackened off in Carthage, though in Rome it became more fierce. Cornelius was sent into exile in the spring of 253 and died there about the middle of the year. Lucius was chosen as his successor.

But peace slowly returned to the church. Gallus was succeeded as emperor by Decius' censor, Valerian, and at first it seemed as though he might not be utterly opposed to Christianity, however much he shared Decius' views about the need to restore Roman morality. The problem of the lapsed had been virtually settled. Hard cases still needed individual attention and a third gathering of bishops in Carthage dealt with some of them. Cyprian himself had had to decide a number of such matters and other bishops would be in the same position.[37] The new council was not, therefore, concerned with policy or fundamental principles. The individual cases, though difficult, were minor problems.

In every way, then, the crisis had been less serious than Cyprian had feared. The persecution was less fierce, less systematic, and shorter than under Decius. The problem of the lapsed had been solved in a way which was generally acceptable to the church as a whole. Even the rival schisms of Maximus and Fortunatus turned out to be less of a danger than they first seemed to be. Maximus's party was, perhaps, never a very serious threat. It was the laxists in Carthage, not the rigorists, who had separatist tendencies. Strict as the average Christian layman in the city might be, he was ready to remain within the congregation and there to urge and demand that the restoration of the lapsed should not be made too easy. Cyprian had to struggle against such men in his determination to be merciful.[38] But even when the allegedly penitent let him down he does not seem to have expected anything more than 'sorrow' from the very people who had opposed his gentleness. Probably Cyprian had been for so long the champion of firmness and discipline that it would be difficult to paint a convincing picture of him as the apostle of antinomianism. The Novatianists survived as a small if belligerent body, with no very great following.

The laxists, on the other hand, having begun as a large and popular movement, vanished comparatively quickly. Cyprian and the second council had drawn their sting. Felicissimus' publicity recoiled on his own head: he announced that twenty-five bishops were coming to consecrate Fortunatus and only a handful turned up.[39] The laity hesitated to take the drastic step of setting up a second bishop in Carthage.[40] Cornelius had refused to support the schismatics. Fortunatus and Felicissimus found themselves virtually without a congregation.[41] As the year 253 ended, then, the whole situation must have seemed unexpectedly hopeful.

7

THE promise, the hope of crises successfully negotiated, which seemed to mark the end of the year 253, did not in fact materialize. Apart from the first eighteen months (and even then he was not without his difficulties) Cyprian was never given any real period of peace in the whole decade of his episcopate. First there were the disputes over his election and the opposition of Novatus. Then came the persecution, and his withdrawal to his hiding-place. There followed the long, complex wrangle over the lapsed, and the settlement of this issue involved him in the Roman quarrels also. Renewed persecution and renewed schism in Carthage followed almost immediately and these had hardly lost their initial sharpness when Cyprian found himself embroiled in a bitter controversy with a brother bishop.

Lucius, Cornelius' successor as bishop of Rome, died early in 254. He had been exiled almost immediately after his election, and his episcopate lasted only a very few months. It would scarcely have been possible, therefore, for him to leave much of a mark on the history of the church. Cyprian wrote him one letter and its tone suggests that he regarded Lucius as a man of faith and courage and that they were on good terms. [1] But by the middle of the year Lucius, in his turn, had been succeeded by Stephen, a man whose personality was as powerful as Cyprian's.

him at once as the true bishop of Rome, Cyprian's reply merely lectured him further on the great advantage of having one's election tested and proved.[7] When Cyprian intervened in Roman affairs to try to persuade the confessors to accept Cornelius, Cornelius himself showed no umbrage. He merely ignored the part Cyprian had played in the affair, writing as if the confessors had come back of their own accord.[8] When the troubles at Rome were at their height, Cyprian sent Cornelius a pretty clear recipe for action, not telling him what to do but laying down what a good bishop would do. 'If some think they can come back to the Church not with prayers but with threats . . . let them be sure that the Church of the Lord stands closed . . . God's bishop, holding fast the gospel and keeping Christ's commands, cannot be conquered though he may be killed.'[9] Pompous, lacking in humour, but very clear about what duty meant for himself and others, Cyprian got into the way of laying down the law. Cornelius preferred to preserve his dignity by evading rather than welcoming a fight. But there are few things more galling for a man than to have his duties spelled out for him, especially when he already knows just what they are. Cyprian's letter to Cornelius congratulating him and praising him for being exiled for the faith ends, less tactfully, by saying that Cyprian has been warned by God that the real crisis was coming soon and that they must both be ready for it.

Lucius was bishop for so short a time that there was not time for a real relationship to develop between him and Cyprian. In the one letter the bishop of Carthage wrote to him exactly the same technique was used. Again Cyprian does not tell Lucius what to do, he describes what he will do and what will happen to him. Cyprian will pray that God will perfect in Lucius the martyr's crown for it is likely that God has brought the bishop of Rome back from exile so that he can be offered as a sacrifice when the brethren are present to witness his death.[10]

All this is worth stressing because it shows why Cyprian and the new Roman bishop were almost bound to clash. Cyprian honestly did not think of himself as interfering, presumptuous or overbearing. This was how he treated himself and he had got into the habit of treating other people in the same way. But it is easy to see why Stephen, who was a very different kind of person from Cornelius, would resent such treatment. It is also easy to see why Cyprian would be taken aback at being resented.

Stephen seems to have been an authoritarian but not a disciplinarian. That is to say, he was just as concerned as was Cyprian himself to maintain the authority of his office as bishop, and as bishop of Rome. But he belonged to the same tradition as Cornelius in that he was generous, and lenient in his attitude to church discipline. He was far less puritanical even than Cyprian had gradually become, and he did not necessarily regard himself as bound by decisions already taken by others. It was precisely this combination of emphasis upon authority with liberality in discipline which brought the two bishops into head-on collision.

The trouble arose in two ways. In Spain two bishops, Martial and Basilides, had acquired certificates stating that they had sacrificed during the persecution, though in fact they had probably not done so. Cyprian and the other African bishops, meeting in the autumn of 254, approved the fact that the Spanish churches had chosen new bishops in their place. They pointed out that even Cornelius had agreed that lapsed bishops could not be restored to office, though they might be readmitted to the church if they showed themselves penitent.[11] But Stephen had apparently sided with the deposed bishops (or had been taken in by them, the Africans thought) and had recognized them as the rightful shepherds of their Spanish flocks.[12] What is particularly significant for the future controversy is that the letter written to Spain by the African bishops enunciates the principle that Christians who do not separate themselves from an unlawful or sinful bishop are polluted by him. 'All those who have been contaminated by the sacrifice of a profane and unrighteous *sacerdos* are bound to sin.'[13] It is probable from the context that the African bishops are thinking of those who participate in the eucharist celebrated by such a man.

The other matter concerned Marcianus, the bishop of Arles in Gaul. Marcianus had adopted a Novatianist line, resolutely refusing pardon to the lapsed, however penitent. The bishop of Lyons wrote to Cyprian to tell him what had happened and also informed him that Stephen knew all about it. The bishop of Rome, however, had apparently taken no action.[14] Cyprian wrote to Stephen in his customary vein: 'Send letters to the province and people of Arles by which means Marcianus may be excommunicated and someone else be substituted for him.' 'The honour of . . . the blessed martyrs [*sic*] Cornelius and

Lucius must be maintained . . .'. 'Tell us plainly who has been put in Marcianus's place at Arles . . .'. It is all very plain and straightforward. Cyprian really does not see how Stephen can hesitate. And he drives it all home with a double-edged barb. Cornelius and Lucius, he writes, had agreed with him about the restoration of the lapsed, 'for there could be no disagreement among us in whom there was one spirit: therefore it is clear that he whom we see to think differently does not hold the truth of the Holy Spirit with the rest [of us].'[15] Does this mean that Marcianus is already virtually excommunicate because he adopts a different policy about the lapsed? Or is it directed at Stephen himself, hinting that he may be outside the Christian consensus?

In this letter Cyprian urged that the Christian bishops as a whole had a pressing duty to care lovingly for those who had been turned away by the harsh Novatianism of men like Marcianus. The great controversial issue was what was to be done with the Novatianists themselves, if they wished to join the church. A large number of such cases must have arisen because the inquiries began to come in thick and fast, beginning with a query from a layman, Magnus. Cyprian replies very firmly indeed that it is necessary for Novatianists to be baptized when they come into the fold because only the true church can give true baptism. He reverts to the argument, already used elsewhere,[16] in which he relies upon an analogy between the Christian ministry and the Jewish priesthood. He applies Old Testament texts literally to the Christian situation[17] and concludes that an unlawful priest cannot do things which please God and will corrupt, contaminate and damn those who follow him. Therefore the sacraments of schismatics are null or actually damaging, and converts from among them must receive proper Christian baptism. This was to be his standpoint throughout the proceedings and he has harsh things to say about those (like Stephen) who are within the church and yet wish to recognize schismatic baptism.[18]

It is obvious that there must already have been some disagreement on the matter and that tempers were already high. The controversy spread. Eighteen bishops of Numidia were the next inquirers. They seem to have practised fresh baptism of schismatics but to have begun to have doubts about the wisdom of the policy. As a result, a gathering of thirty-one bishops met in Carthage in 255 and sent an answer to the Numidians. The synod was not unanimous but the reply sets out Cyprian's consistent argument. Schismatics are outside the church and do not, therefore, possess the Holy Spirit. What they do not possess they cannot give.

The question arises, in view of the doubts of the Numidians and the lack of unanimity in the council, whether there really was a firm North African tradition which demanded 'rebaptism'.[19] There cannot, in the nature of the case, be full and conclusive proof that this had been the invariable and immemorial custom. But Tertullian had certainly maintained that those outside the true church[20] could not administer a true baptism.[21] The council held early in the third century, the first thing we really know about in the institutional life of the African Church, had also decided that heretics must be baptized afresh.[22] On the other hand Cyprian, though he cites the African tradition, does not make overmuch of tradition and custom in general, preferring other arguments.[23] It is probable, therefore, that in Africa and Numidia there was a school of thought which had always maintained the necessity of baptizing converts from heresy or schism, but that this had not been a universal opinion. Hence the doubts and hesitations of so many people.

Still the queries came in. Quintus, a bishop in Mauretania, asked what the right policy was and Cyprian sent a reply which hints that Stephen was beginning to take a strong line on Roman tradition. Cyprian does not say so in so many words but he rejects any argument based upon custom and the primacy of Peter. 'Nor must we prescribe this on the basis of custom alone, but prevail by reason. For Peter, whom the Lord chose first and on whom he built his Church, did not claim or usurp anything for himself insolently and arrogantly when Paul later argued with him about circumcision. . . .'[24] It looks as though Stephen has begun to try and assert his rank and Cyprian is resenting it.

Perhaps to cool his own temper, perhaps to restrain others, Cyprian wrote two works at about this time. One dealt with the need for patience and the other with jealousy and envy. As usual he is writing for himself as much as anything but there are passages which ring peculiarly aptly under the circumstances. Urging that those who are in Christ must follow his example in turning the other cheek, Cyprian says:

> Peter also, upon whom by the Lord's generosity the Church
> was founded, lays it down in his epistle and says, Christ
> suffered for us, leaving you an example that you should
> follow his footsteps, who did no sin neither was deceit found
> in his mouth; who when he was reviled, reviled not again;
> when he suffered, threatened not but gave himself up to him
> that judged him unjustly.[25]

This is the kind of primacy Cyprian expected in Peter's
successor, a primacy in gentleness and long-suffering, not the
pulling of rank. The requirement for eminence in the church is
that one should be Christ-like, and it is a shock to find an
eminent servant of Christ claiming the power to lay down the
law for everyone else.[26] One would have supposed, of course,
that Cyprian was the very embodiment of precisely this fault.
Perhaps he could only see how un-christian such an
authoritarianism was when it emanated from others. Perhaps he
had convinced himself that he really had ceased to be that kind
of person. Perhaps he merely resented the fact that there was
someone else who intended to treat him as he had treated
others. At all events it made him realize how unpleasant it was.
Only the peacemakers, he wrote, can be called the sons of God,
answering to the likeness of God the Father and of Christ.[27]
Neither Cyprian nor Stephen found it easy to answer to that
likeness.

In the spring of 256 a new council of bishops met at Carthage
to discuss the whole baptismal issue again. There were seventy-
one of them and they came from Numidia as well as Africa.
This time their decision was unanimous. There is only one
baptism, that of the catholic church. Those who come from
other bodies are not, indeed, rebaptized, for what they have had
is not baptism. They are baptized for the first and only time. To
use Cyprian's language, reflecting his concept of the church as
the one area where the power of evil did not rule, they come
from the tainted, adulterous water, to be washed and made holy
by the water of salvation and truth.[28]

The council sent Stephen a letter which, while it opened with
the conventional expressions of affection, was uncompromising
and even fierce in tone. It ended with the significant words:

But we know that there are some who will not lightly drop what they have once accepted and who do not easily change their minds but retain certain peculiarities which they have adopted, while keeping the bond of peace and concord with their colleagues. Concerning this we neither use force nor impose a law on anyone, since each bishop has freedom to make up his own mind in the administration of the Church, remembering that he will have to give an account of his conduct to the Lord.[29]

It is worth taking note of the three points made in this closing statement. Variation in custom from place to place, the right of the bishop to judge for himself, the importance of 'the bond of peace' which is stronger than difference of opinion, are all crucial to Cyprian's thought. It was the argument which he built upon these three points which enabled him both to assert his own opinions and to maintain his freedom in the face of Stephen's claims.

After the bishops had gone home again yet another inquiry came in. Jubaianus, a bishop in Mauretania, wrote to Cyprian and enclosed a document he had come across which put the Roman point of view. Cyprian's reply[30] is, perhaps, the most thorough of his various attempts to thrash out the theological issues involved. He asserts that the practice of baptizing heretics afresh is traditional in Africa. It is a right practice because, after all, baptism involves the faith of the baptized in God, Father, Son and Spirit. If heretics have no right belief in God how can they be rightly baptized? There is plainly a reference here to the actual rite of baptism which contained a recitation of the creed.[31] There is a certain logic in maintaining that heretics cannot possibly proclaim the faith in the same sense as true believers and that this invalidates their baptism. But that argument would not cover the case of schismatics who were orthodox in theology.

Whether he has perceived this flaw in the argument or not, Cyprian does bolster it up with another favourite one. Baptism and the remission of sins can only be given by those appointed in the church (and there is the familiar reference to Peter 'on whom the church is built'). False priests (as in the Old Testament) can do nothing. Penitence and forgiveness, the laying on of hands by the bishop after baptism, martyrdom as baptism in one's own blood, all these are examined in relation to baptism itself. Again and again Cyprian hammers home the point that nothing done by the heretic, who stands outside the church, has the slightest value in the sight of God. At last he comes to his great crescendo. If there is no salvation outside the church, the heretic is stained rather than washed by his false baptism, is piling up new sins instead of getting rid of old ones. 'And so baptism cannot be common to us and to the heretics, to whom not God the Father, nor Christ the Son, nor the Holy Spirit, nor the faith, nor the very Church itself, is common.'[32] Page after page comes from Cyprian's pen and then he ends with an (ironical?) reference to the briefness of his reply and a restatement of the theme which concluded the letter of the council to Stephen. He also encloses some of the other relevant documents and his treatise on patience. Cyprian has no wish, he says, to lay down the law to anyone. Each bishop must be free to exercise his own judgment. It is the bond of peace, in spite of differences, which holds the church together. Quoting I Corinthians 11:6, he reminds Jubaianus: 'If any man, however, is thought to be contentious, we have no such custom, neither the Church of God.'

The quotation doesn't quite fit. It is as if Cyprian is trying to say that the one custom a Christian cannot have is quarrelsomeness. Patience, love, concord, cooperation, gentleness are what really matter. But he has made his points with great firmness, nevertheless. And his argument can really only be understood against the liturgical practice of his day. In the ceremony of baptism the new Christian came out of the water to have the bishop's hands laid upon his head. The latter action was, perhaps, identified with the gift of the Spirit.[33] But baptism was also connected with the remission of sins: this was part of the meaning of the sacrament.[34] The forgiveness of sins, subsequent to baptism was inevitably thought of as being in some sense a parallel act, almost a second baptism.[35] But sinners readmitted to the Christian fellowship were restored, not by a new baptism in water, but by the laying on of the bishop's hands after a period of penitence.[36] The lapsed, who as apostates had denied Christ, were also readmitted in this way in accordance with the decisions taken by the councils of bishops. Heretics who left the church after baptism could be regarded as virtual apostates, deniers of Christ. Such people, having been baptized before baptized before their apostasy, could quite simply be treated like the lapsed and could be readmitted by the laying on of hands.[37] They were being treated as penitent sinners. It was all neat and logical.

Those who, like Stephen, maintained that baptism was baptism even if administered outside the true church, argued that the laying on of hands was always a sufficient means of reconciling heretics to the church. This Cyprian would not allow. These were not being *reconciled* for they had *never* been part of the church. They were being baptized for the first time, for the first time being brought into the church. Therefore they must be baptized fully and completely. The laying on of hands could not suffice. Either the heretic had been baptized in water and had received the laying on of hands, already, in the false church from which he came, or he had received neither. The two are inseparable. 'Either he could obtain both privileges by his faith outside [the church], or he who has been outside has received neither.'[38]

Part of the trouble in the controversy between Cyprian and Stephen may, then, have been the result of a confusion over the two different but related acts of laying on of hands in baptism and in the reconciliation of sinners. Stephen, thinking of it as reconciliation of erring Christians, thought it sufficient that the bishop should lay his hands upon them, signifying their new solidarity with the church. Cyprian, regarding them as being utterly outside the church, believed that they must be initiated into it and, in initiation, water and the laying on of hands were inseparable.

But part of the trouble was also a matter of personalities. A deputation of African bishops had gone to Rome after the council of 256. Stephen refused to see them.[39] Instead he made it known that he would refuse to regard those who rebaptized as being any longer part of the church. This decision was published in the eastern half of the Mediterranean world also and provoked a long and furious reply from Firmilian, bishop of Caesarea in Cappadocia. He wrote to Cyprian,[40] encouraging him with the assurance that the church in the east also refused to recognize heretical or schismatic baptism, making some disparaging remarks about Stephen's un-christian temper, and underlining the comic fact that one bishop who excommunicated everyone else, would find that it was really himself who was excommunicated.

in the east; he had also extended his influence further and further across North Africa, first in Numidia then in Mauretania also. He had become much more than bishop of Carthage.

8

THE best known of all the books which Cyprian wrote is his treatise on the unity of the church, *De Ecclesiae Catholicae Unitate*. In the twentieth century Christians have been deeply concerned with the ecumenical movement, the various attempts to reunite the separated churches and the whole question of unity across racial and cultural as well as denominational boundaries. At the same time many of the early hopes and enthusiasms of the ecumenical movement have evaporated. Schemes have gone wrong or come to nothing. The general disenchantment with institutions has reacted upon proposals for uniting ecclesiastical organizations. Even where several Christian traditions have been reunited, it often seems to have made very little difference in practice. The combination of anxious concern and deep disappointment means that one can hardly avoid hoping that Cyprian may have something to say which may be relevant to our own situation. So much of the general condition of third-century Christian life is as different as it possibly could be from that of the twentieth. Yet there are ways in which Cyprian seems, at least at first sight, to adopt attitudes not entirely dissimilar from those of contemporary Christians. His very reaction to the church of which he became and organizational structures do not matter. Nor is he, equally obviously, thinking of a unity which depends on doctrinal agreement. Neither of our modern attitudes will apply. The only other possibility seems to be that he believed that, provided he and Stephen were both rightful bishops, the unity of the church could be maintained even if they disagreed about the basic concept of what that unity was. They were both lawful occupants of their sees. They were both bishops. They were both within the boundaries of the visible church. They both possessed the Spirit.

Can this be what Cyprian meant? It is clear that he holds the highest view of the bishop's office. From the very first he had insisted on the necessity for discipline and obedience, which implied that he had the right to require these things, even from those of the highest repute: virgins and confessors. He expects the clergy to obey him. He believes himself to be called to his office by the judgment of God and this gives him an enormous authority. When the laxist clergy and the confessors began to restore the lapsed, Cyprian's chief complaint was that they were undermining that authority. This was perhaps his principal reason for insisting that nothing be done till peace came and this was certainly the most consistent feature in Cyprian's policy at the time.

We have already seen how he applied Old Testament texts to the bishop's office.[8] *Sacerdos* is the word he usually uses for a bishop. Passages which initially referred to the Levitical priesthood are transferred to the Christian ministry. This is not as odd as it may seem at first sight, nor was it merely a gratuitous attempt to magnify the episcopate. The influence of Judaism was strong in Carthaginian Christianity, and in the Punic religion there had been preserved a priestly caste very like that of the Levites.[9] Such a ministry was a living tradition in Cyprian's world. It would be natural, if not wholly justifiable, to assume that the Christian ministry could be thought of in the same terms. But once this was done then inevitably one would begin to think in terms also of the lawful, true, valid priesthood required to perform the lawful, true and valid rites. Inevitably the Old Testament examples of the awful fate which befell those who presumed to take it upon themselves to perform priestly functions would suggest themselves. Cyprian made full use of them.[10]

Again, since the Old Testament priesthood needed to be the true and authentic priesthood so as to perform acceptable rites, it was another easy step to the argument that unlawful Christian clergy could not administer proper sacraments. It is perfectly consistent for Cyprian to argue, as he frequently does in the rebaptism controversy, that an heretical minister cannot baptize or celebrate the eucharist. Nor is it a surprise to discover that Cyprian believed that bishops have other important functions as intermediaries. In *De Lapsis* he spoke of '. . . the satisfaction and remission, made by the bishops, . . . acceptable to the Lord . . .'.[11] He is presumably speaking of the bishop's actions in reconciling penitents. It is clear that he sees himself and his colleagues as performing that which is necessary to preserve a proper relationship between God and his people, and as endowed with great power from God.

Yet this is never thought of as a personal possession. Cyprian always talks of the bishop's authority as being within the church. What makes a bishop the rightful bishop is the choice made by the clergy, people and other bishops. If the church is in the bishop, as well as the bishop in the church, this is because the bishop is the focal point for the church's power as well as its life. The bishop ought always to act with his people.[12] And this is perfectly logical, for the church is a visible concrete body and outside the church the bishop, like anyone else, is nothing. In the 'rebaptism' controversy the whole point of Cyprian's argument is that the true bishop possesses (and can give) the Spirit because he is within the true church. His concept of the relationship between church and ministry is, therefore, not as mechanical and juridical as his severest critics have alleged. The bishop must stand within the reality of the corporate church and therefore within the reality of the power of the Holy Spirit. This power alone can achieve anything against sin, evil and death. The bishop is the focus for its operation.

Cyprian also clearly believed that he was personally inspired by the Spirit on certain occasions, as well as empowered by him in the performance of sacramental rites. The importance he attached to dreams as a vehicle by which God spoke to him, and the complete certainty with which he passed on these revelations to others, is proof of this. It is possible that he thought of this inspiration as present in every bishop.[13] He told Stephen, before the rebaptism controversy, that if some bishops disagreed with the majority it was because they were somehow apart from the truth and unity of the one Spirit.[14] On the other hand there were times when he seems to have thought that God had revealed things to him but not to some other bishops, otherwise there would have been little point in his writing to Cornelius to warn him that the greatest crisis was about to come.[15] One cannot, therefore, be entirely certain how far this personal inspiration came to him *qua* bishop or whether this is a case in which Cyprian combined in his own person the institutional authority of the organized church and the prophetic, inspirational traditions of Africa.[16]

But, of course, the corporate nature of the bishop's authority in the church was also bound up with this very matter of the relations between the bishops. In part, as we have seen, the whole concept was forced on Cyprian by the practical necessity of arriving at a common policy on the problem of the lapsed. To say that the unity of the church was partly a matter of bishops reaching agreement among themselves was not so much a theological statement about a quasi-mystical concept of episcopate as a reflection of the actual situation. A common episcopal mind was the only way in which the threatening divisions in the church were likely to be healed. The practical advantages of the successive North African councils underlined this fact, and the odd alliance between Cyprian and Cornelius at the same time made it plain that a 'common mind' did not mean complete uniformity in theology.[17] The way in which the practical and the theological overlap and intertwine is very obvious here. He writes as if agreement will be achieved simply because it ought to be achieved.[18] Sometimes he even gives the impression that, while he is crystal clear about the way in which a bishop's authority operates in every other particular, he has never really thought out how that authority stands in relation to other bishops.[19]

The explanation may be that practical reality and theological truth were not radically separated in Cyprian's thought. The hard facts of experience and the exigencies of successive crises did more to develop Cyprian's view of the authority of the episcopate and the nature of Christian unity than any abstract theological speculation. But the Holy Spirit was, for Cyprian, also one of the hard facts of experience. There was a real sense in which the Spirit guided and directed the bishops and held

them with the bonds of concord in spite of their differences.
Cyprian did say that two bishops could disagree about an
important matter of doctrine without breaking the unity of the
church, provided they were both rightful occupants of their sees
and thus within the visible church and the realm of the Spirit.
But he meant it in a sense rather different from what it seems at
first sight.

One needs to ask the further question: what did Cyprian
believe was the fundamental unity so strong that the widest
theological differences could yet be reconciled with a very
concrete concept of a single church? This seems to be a
question which, on the whole, the historians have not asked.
Even where they have recognized that Cyprian's controversy
with Stephen was a theological one, they have persisted in
treating it as though it were not. Thus one of the great
authorities, expounding Cyprian's view of the episcopate, says,
'A bishop could not then resist their united voice [i.e. the united
voice of the body of bishops] without hardihood, but if he did,
he was unassailable *unless* viciousness of life or *false* doctrine
were patent in his life or teaching.'[20]

This is surely to miss the whole point. So far as Cyprian was
concerned Stephen *was* teaching false doctrine. In a savage
piece of sarcasm he wrote:

> An excellent and lawful tradition is indeed put forward by
> our brother Stephen's teaching! He supplies us with a
> sufficient authority. . . . To this depth of evil has God's
> Church, Christ's spouse sunk, that she must follow the
> example of heretics; that light must borrow its order for
> celebrating the heavenly sacraments from darkness; and
> Christians must copy Antichrists.[21]

Stephen had said that even the heretics do not rebaptize.
Cyprian felt that to cite the example of heretics was to be worse
than a heretic. Moreover Firmilian's letter said quite
categorically that Stephen's teaching was very great error[22] and
it is difficult to know what this can mean if it does not imply
false doctrine. It is true that Cyprian seems to draw a distinction
between the 'error' of Stephen and the 'heresy' of, for instance,
the Montanists. One could try and evade the difficulty by
arguing that error is not as dreadful as heresy. But sometimes
Cyprian speaks of heresy when he ought, by modern standards,

to use the term 'schism' (i.e. of the Novatianists). In fact, he often seems to be more upset by schism than by doctrinal error.

It is true that the early church often made the same distinction that we do, using 'schism' to describe a breach of unity which did not involve a breach in doctrine. But the distinction was not consistently nor precisely made,[23] and, in fact, Cyprian seems to distinguish between 'error' on the one hand and 'heresy and schism' on the other. All his letters on the subject of heretical baptism seem to imply that Stephen is very seriously in error. On the other hand the word 'heretic' is used indiscriminately to describe all those who have separated themselves from the church, whether they have done so on any distinctively theological ground or not. In other words Cyprian seems to behave as though it were possible to be in doctrinal error and yet not be a heretic. To separate oneself from the church, whether one was in doctrinal error or not, was a very different matter. One was deliberately breaking the church's unity.

This is the point at which the controversial character of *De Unitate* is of crucial importance, because it makes it difficult to use that treatise to settle the argument. The question is, what does separating oneself from the church mean? *De Unitate,* or rather the vital section of it, exists in two versions. One of them, usually called the 'Primacy Text' because it seems to assert the primacy of the bishop of Rome, seems to suggest that separating oneself from that bishop is separating oneself from the church. The other version, which seems to have been the version known in North Africa itself and is called the *textus receptus,* does not. The easiest way to compare the two is to see them in parallel columns. The Primacy Text is in the left hand column, the *textus receptus* in the right hand one.[24]

But if anyone considers those things carefully, he will need no long discourse or arguments. The proof is simple and convincing, being summed up in a matter of fact. The Lord says to Peter: 'I say to thee, that thou art Peter and upon this rock I will build my Church, and the gates of hell shall not overcome it. I will give to thee the keys of the kingdom of heaven. And what thou shalt bind upon earth shall be bound also in heaven, and whatsover thou shalt loose on earth shall be loosed also in heaven.'

And he says to him again after the resurrection: 'Feed my sheep.' It is on him that He builds the Church, and to him that He entrusts the sheep to feed. And although He assigns a like power to all the Apostles, yet He founded a single Chair, thus establishing by His own authority the source and hallmark of the [Church's] oneness. No doubt the others were all that Peter was, but a primacy is given to Peter, and it is [thus] made clear that there is but one Church and one Chair. So too, even if they are all shepherds, we are shown but one flock which is to be fed by all the Apostles in common accord. If a man does not hold fast to this oneness of Peter, does he imagine that he still holds the faith? If he deserts the Chair of Peter upon whom the Church was built, has he still confidence that he is in the Church?

It is on one man that He builds the Church, and although He assigns a like power to all the Apostles after His resurrection, saying. 'As the Father hath sent me, I also send you . . . Receive ye the Holy Spirit: if you forgive any man his sins, they shall be forgiven him; if you retain any man's, they shall be retained, yet, in order that the oneness might be unmistakable, He established by His own authority a source for that oneness having its origin in one man alone. No doubt the other Apostles were all that Peter was, endowed with equal dignity and power, but the start comes from him alone, in order to show that the Church of Christ is unique. Indeed this oneness of the Church is figured in the Canticle of Canticles when the Holy Spirit, speaking in Our Lord's name, says: 'One is my dove, my perfect one: to her mother she is the only one, the darling of her womb'. If a man does not hold fast to this oneness of the Church, does he imagine that he still holds the faith?

If he resists and withstands
the Church, has he
still confidence that he
is in the Church, when
the blessed Apostle Paul
gives us this very teaching
and points to the
mystery of Oneness saying:
'One body and one Spirit,
one hope of your calling,
one Lord, one Faith, one
Baptism, one God'?
5. Now this oneness we
must hold to firmly and
insist on—especially
we who are bishops and
exercise authority in the
Church—so as to
demonstrate that
the episcopal power
is one and undivided too.
Let none mislead the
brethren with a lie,
let none corrupt the true
content of the faith by a
faithless perversion of
the truth.

The authority of the bishops forms a unity, of which each
holds his part in its totality.

Opinions have differed, radically and sometimes violently, on
how to explain these variations in the text. The Primacy Text
has been roundly denounced as a naïve forgery.[25] It has also
been argued that if the 'interpolations' were really authentic this
would involve 'both the argument of *De Unitate* and the
subsequent conduct of its author in a mass of contradictions'.[26]
Other scholars have maintained just as vigorously that the
Primacy Text was the original. Now, however, there seems to be
a greater degree of unanimity. Perhaps Cyprian wrote both
versions!
Disagreement still exists about which version is the earlier.

Either the *textus receptus* was written at the time of the first council held at Carthage to determine the church's policy towards the lapsed, while the later version was aimed at the attempt by Novatian to claim the episcopal chair at Rome; or the Primary Text is the original, while the other version was a modified form designed to counter the exaggerated claims of Stephen. That is to say that it is possible that *De Unitate* was meant not as a defence of the primacy of Rome but to maintain the authority of the true as against the false bishop of Rome. When Stephen later claimed an authority over the whole church, Cyprian was compelled to modify some of the statements he had made about the centrality of Peter, because Stephen was reading more into his work than he had intended.[27]

If it is possible, now, to get away from some of this controversy, it may be worth noting that reference to Peter is a favourite device of Cyprian's. He obviously thought of Peter as a symbol of unity and authority (or of the unity of authority) long before the quarrel with Stephen ever began. Writing to the lapsed from his hiding place during the first persecution, Cyprian reminds them that the name and title of 'the church' cannot be claimed by any group of people, even the majority. Peter was the symbol of the church's unity and of its authority to bind and loose. The bishops are similar symbols of authority and unity. If loosing is to be done it must be done by the bishop as Peter, the rock of unity. But the bishop acts not by himself but with the clergy and those who have remained faithful.[28]

The same sort of argument appears in a letter to the laity warning them against the Five Presbyters. Again the fundamental point is that authority cannot be either divided or self-made. It is given by God and is by nature one. There is one God, one church, one chair, founded on the rock by the word of the Lord.[29] The context in which this statement appears is Cyprian's favourite analogy with the valid, rightful Levitical priesthood. Though he does not mention Peter by name, Peter is plainly hovering just out of sight.

In the correspondence with Cornelius a new element is introduced, the relationship between the Roman and African bishops. As we have seen, Cyprian recognizes, as a matter of plain fact, the greater importance of Rome.[30] He also seems to recognize that Rome was the source from which mission took the gospel to other parts of the (Western) world. He calls Rome

the womb or root of the catholic church.[31] When he writes to
Cornelius about Fortunatus and Felicissimus and their activities
he is highly indignant that they dare to send schismatic letters to
the chair of Peter and to the chief church from which episcopal
(sacerdotal) unity takes its source.[32] In other words he seems to
be saying, at this point, that the Roman bishop is the prototype.
The Roman church is the mother church: the others come from
her. The Roman bishop is Peter: the other bishops are images or
types of Peter. If we remember how Cyprian always took the
line that the higher one stood in the church the more perfect one
was required to be,[33] there seems to be little here that conflicts
with the Primacy version of *De Unitate*. Even Cyprian's
reference to the feeding of the flock would fit. The primacy of
Rome lies in its being the pastoral pattern, the prototypical
Peter, the symbol of unitive authority, the source from which
other bishops and churches came and on whom they are
modelled.

But we have also to remember that Cyprian changed his
mind on other crucial matters, notably the treatment of the
lapsed. In the rebaptism controversy he continues to point to
Peter as the symbol of the one authority. But now there are
times when this is said on a note of savage sarcasm. He quotes
the real Peter against the symbolic Peter.[34] He rejects the
primacy in the sense of a rank which can be used to force other
bishops, other Peters, to fall into line.[35] But he continues to use
Peter as an argument to show that, as Christ chose one man
first of all to receive authority, so authority in the church is
God-given and unitary, belonging to the true priesthood.[36]

This does represent something of a change in attitude
towards the Roman bishop, but it is not entirely inconsistent
with what Cyprian had said before. Just as he sees each bishop
as a Peter, symbol and source of unity, yet denies that a bishop
can act apart from the church, so he will not allow that
Stephen's character as an archetypal Peter gives him the right to
act alone. He resents what he feels is Stephen's failure to be
what God has called him to be. But he does not abandon the
whole concept of Peter as type and symbol. Moreover Cyprian
was essentially pragmatic. If a theory did not measure up to the
hard facts of the situation, he saw no harm in modifying it, so it
is entirely possible that the *textus receptus* may represent the
sort of modification that Cyprian might have introduced into

the original in the heat of his controversy with Stephen. Peter as type of unitive authority is still there, but the primacy of Rome, in the sense of superior rank and power, is carefully cut out.

Obviously there can be no conclusive proof that this is the correct explanation, but it is plausible enough to serve as a working hypothesis. For the truth is that Peter and the primacy may not be so tremendously important for understanding *De Unitate* after all, even though one dare not discuss Cyprian's treatise without first acknowledging the complexities of the textual problem.

The argument of *De Unitate* goes something like this: subtle temptations are a greater danger to the church than open attack. Therefore it is essential that the church at all times cling consciously to Christ's commands. Heresies and schisms are a subtle deceit of the devil who attempts to make a counterfeit church. But there is only one church, and Christ's promise to one man (Peter) is the sign of this. It is the duty of all, and especially the bishops, to maintain the exuberant unity of the church. But the unity of the church proceeds from the unity of God: to divide it is sin. The New Israel cannot (unlike the Old Israel) be rent asunder, for each Christian has put on Christ. There can only be one church since the church is a family. The Christian pattern of life is meekness, love and simplicity, not violence and separation. Heresies exist because God permits sin and so that the faithful may be sifted. But false bishops are false prophets, and since they are cut off from the source of life, they cannot give life. Since heresies and schisms cut themselves off from the unity and peace of Christ, Christ cannot be with them. The church is not an assembly of people who *call* themselves Christ's but is those who obey his commands. Prayer is ineffective if it is rooted in strife, bitterness and an unwillingness to forgive. Even willingness to suffer as a martyr cannot compensate for a lack of love and humility. Since God is love, to deny love (and peace and unity) is to deny God and be separated from him. No mighty and miraculous acts are worth anything unless they spring from the love and unity of the two great commandments. Heretics are self-centred, self-willed agents of the devil's attempt to destroy the church. Such men cannot be an example of Christ to Christ's flock. If they attempt to minister as God's priests they are presumptuous. Heresy is unlike other sins since the heretic is too proud to admit his sin.

Even the man who has suffered for the faith may be led by pride into schism. To be a hero or a leader in the church is no guarantee therefore that a man may not err. It is the duty of the Christian to win such men back, but if they are incorrigible they must be abandoned. In that case the church is not really divided, for such men are outside the church. Within the church men must be peacemakers, filled with the spirit of love and unity. Then the church's prayers and ministrations are effective. But Christians tend to forget the need for unity, as they forget the need for charity and faith. Christians ought to be ready for Christ's coming, not foolishly falling into the devil's traps.

Several points emerge at once. In the first place, when taken in the context of the treatise as a whole, the place of Peter is seen not to look very large. He is the symbol and the source of the unity of the church, it is true, but this seems to be used by Cyprian chiefly to prove that there *can* only be one church; that is to say, to prove the uniqueness rather than the unity of the church.[37] It is true that it is possible to interpret one sentence of the Primacy Text to mean that those who are not in communion with Rome may be outside the church, but the same text can just as easily be interpreted as if Cyprian were speaking of the real historical Peter rather than of the see of Rome.[38] The important thing is that the whole matter of Peter's primacy and even of the authority of bishops occupies such a small part of the argument of the book as a whole.

No doubt the conventional exposition of Cyprian's theory of unity and the episcopate is correct in asserting that Cyprian regarded the bishops as the 'glue' of the church. After all Cyprian said of the church that it '. . . is catholic and one, not cut or divided, but everywhere connected and joined by the cement of bishops who cohere with one another.'[39] He says this in a context which is particularly illuminating. He was defending himself against a charge that he was a cause of division. His reply was that Peter is an example not only of the unity and authority but also of the faithfulness of the church. The argument depends on the passage in St John's Gospel where Christ asks the disciples if they also will go away, and Peter replies, 'Lord, to whom shall we go?' If Peter, notorious for denying Christ, could be used as a symbol of constancy on the basis of a single text, then plainly Cyprian was not talking about

the real, historical Peter. He was using a typological interpretation of the text of scripture to make his point.

The point in this case is that Peter cleaves to Christ and so
does the church. So also do the Christian people cleave to the
bishop. The strict logic of the argument really depends on the
faithful being equated with Peter and the bishop with Christ.
But this Cyprian does not press, indicating once more that one
must not take his typology too seriously. For just as one expects
him to say that the existence of the church depends on the
bishop, he produces instead the much more complete statement
that 'the bishop is in the Church and the Church in the
bishop'.[40]

Of course Cyprian believed, just as Ignatius had believed,
that 'if anyone is not with the bishop then he is not within the
church'.[41] He believed that there could be no eucharist and no
baptism except those performed by the bishop or his delegate.[42]
Ignatius's saving clause ('or one to whom [the bishop] commits
it') plays a larger part, perforce, in Cyprian's thinking, but
basically the concept is the same. It is the bishop whose
authority is needed because the bishop is the one person in
whom the unity of the church can clearly be seen. How it is
possible to have the church where the unity is deliberately
rejected, Cyprian cannot understand.

But if pope and bishop play, after all, a small part in *De
Unitate,* other matters emerge as tremendously important. First
of all there is the point already noted, that Cyprian is clearly
thinking of the church as an obvious, existing unity. Heresy and
schism are hateful because they are a *departure from* that unity.
It is the *act of separation* which is the dreadful sin. When
Cyprian urged Stephen to excommunicate the Novatianists in
Gaul[43] it was because they had separated themselves already.

Then, too, we have already noted that Cyprian drew no hard
and fast distinction between heresy and schism. It was the
presumption involved in setting up 'another church' which upset
him, far more than the holding of unorthodox beliefs. There
were 'heretics' who not only taught false doctrines but also set
themselves up as an alternative church, and there were those
like Stephen, who were 'in error', but who must be kept within
the church at almost any cost. This was not simply because
Stephen was bishop of *Rome,* but because so long as the two
bishops could continue in communion with one another there

was some hope of agreement, especially where the Spirit was at work. Excommunication was to be avoided, except where deliberate schism demanded it, because honest disagreement does not in itself disrupt unity. The church is to Cyprian a dynamic, not a static, unit. The church grows, develops, proliferates exuberantly. Something must hold it together because the branch without the tree, the stream cut off from the source, is lifeless. But what is needed to hold the exuberant unity of the church together is more than a static agreement on matters of doctrine.

It must be asked whether the conventional view is right. Did Cyprian believe that it was the formal connection between bishop and bishop which maintained unity, even where there was wide divergence in doctrine? Did Cyprian really think that he and Stephen could agree to differ on vital matters of faith, provided that they could preserve a formal communion based on the rightful occupation of the see? This hypothesis only partly fits the facts. Cyprian was distressed about heresy proper, just as he was distressed about Stephen's 'error'. But he was equally distressed by the pride and presumption which breaks the unity of the church, whether this manifested itself in the departure of the schismatics or in Stephen's threat to excommunicate the rest of the church. He was certainly concerned with juridical questions and with structure, administration and organization. But he also saw that there were much deeper issues involved.

There is a hidden theme running all the way through *De Unitate* which holds it together. Cyprian begins by saying that Christians are to defeat the subtler temptations of the devil by holding Christ's commands. He quotes John 15:14, 'If you do what I command you, I call you no longer servants but friends.' Christ's command in that context is, 'Love one another as I have loved you.' Cyprian does not quote these words, but the implication is there. Similarly, Christ's promise to Peter, the sign of unity, is also set in the context of the question, 'Simon, son of John, lovest thou me?' though again Cyprian does not explicitly quote this part of the passage. Nevertheless, when he goes on to speak of the unity of the church and the bishop's duty to maintain it, the framework within which his argument is set is one of the duty of love.

The unity of the church, Cyprian says, stems from the unity

of God. Once again he does not actually quote John 17:11, but he asserts that the church is one as the Trinity is one. It is the putting on of Christ that makes Christians one, for they all put on the same Christ and he is the Christ of humility, peace and love. Again and again in *De Unitate,* unity, peace and love are linked together. This is a pastoral rather than an abstract concept. Unity is the concord of real, practical peace and love between Christians. If it is broken, prayer becomes ineffective. One is reminded forcefully of the agonizing dreams which tortured Cyprian in hiding and which taught him that his bitterly divided flock could not pray effectively for peace.[44] There is only one church: if it is divided it is not the church. Heresy and schism are hateful because they break up the concord. The distinctive thing about a heretic is not his false doctrine; this is hardly mentioned. To be a heretic is to be full of pride, strife, presumption and bitterness. It is the rending, tearing significance of both heresy and schism which Cyprian is concerned with. Such a spirit is the opposite of the humble love on which real unity is based. A man with such a spirit, Cyprian points out, cannot be an example to Christ's flock. This is a familiar theme. It is the sort of thing he had said to the virgins, the confessors and the clergy. The Christian spirit of humility, love and peace is the true example, and it is also that which makes prayer effective. The greatest danger is that Christians may forget this. So the treatise ends, as it began, with a warning about the devil's subtlety. The real point emerges at last: Cyprian is desperately afraid that Christian love has become lukewarm.

De Unitate is not, therefore, really a book about pope and bishops. It is a book about the need to love. The key passages quoted from the gospels are passages where the Christian duty of obedience is set in a context of love. That the context itself is not quoted does not greatly matter. We know that Cyprian had a thorough knowledge of the text of scripture and could quote it from memory, easily and extensively.[45] He knew what he was doing, as the rest of the treatise with its refrain of love, peace, concord makes clear.

It is not enough, then, to say that Cyprian believed that the unity of the church depends on the bishops. The idea that this was a formal matter of office and communion and of 'agreeing to differ' within that framework does not really account fully for

Cyprian's thought. The bishop is, indeed, the centre of unity. He is both the unifying point for his own diocese and the link with the rest of the church. But disagreement on *matters of doctrine* need not break the unity within or without the diocese, provided the love is strong enough. In other words, the bishop's function as centre and symbol of unity is not merely a function of office, it is a relationship of love. It is a personal, pastoral relationship with his own people because he is Peter who was commanded to feed the flock of Christ. Of course, this does not mean, for Cyprian, that it is a relationship of easy-going sentimentality. To love Christ's flock and feed it included, besides the quite literal duty to give money and food, the duty to instruct and to command. Christians must be told what the demands of the faith are. It is part of love to do this firmly and unequivocally.[46] Love is a disciplined and uncompromising thing, like Christ's love for the rich young ruler.[47]

The same sort of love, personal and pastoral, binds one bishop to another. There is a bond of concord which holds them together in spite of differences. Several times in his letters Cyprian restates this theme.[48] Whenever he refers to the unity of the bishops in the Holy Spirit, 'joined by the bond of mutual concord',[49] his language evokes Ephesians 4:2f., '. . . with all lowliness and meekness, with patience, forbearing one another in love, eager to maintain the unity of the Spirit in the bond of peace'.[50] Again this is simply not a juridical concept. It is love or the Holy Spirit, the love of God shed abroad, which is strong enough to hold together the exuberant life of the church. Cyprian and Stephen ought to be able to disagree and yet maintain unity not because of a formal communion and a canonically lawful occupation of their sees, but because they strive to obey the command to 'love one another as I have loved you'. A dynamic relationship, rather than a static one, would allow them to grow together in spite of differences. The tragedy was that they did not do so.[51]

The controversy between Cyprian and Stephen was never settled in the sense of a formal decision being taken at a council of the whole church. Tacitly, Christian opinion moved gradually towards Stephen's point of view. The idea that the Holy Spirit was at work only within some precisely defined 'true' church was abandoned. Baptism was recognized as baptism, even if performed by heretics and schismatics, so long as water and the name of the Trinity were used. Or, at least, this was true in the west. In the east the tradition that orthodox belief is necessary for the valid performance of the sacraments has, in some measure, survived. It survived even more vigorously for a short while in Cyprian's own North Africa. In the fourth century the Donatist movement took their stand on what they claimed to be Cyprian's teaching.[52] They argued that a bishop who committed apostasy automatically ceased to be within the true church and was therefore no longer a bishop able to perform the sacraments or give the Holy Spirit. The resulting schism had a great many sociological and political causes as well but it led, in the end, to the acceptance in the west of Stephen's rather than Cyprian's doctrine.

In the west, also, the church as a whole moved towards Stephen's view of authority and unity. The papacy became the centre and focus of both until the sixteenth century. Those who then rejected papal authority did so on theological grounds very different from those of Cyprian, and his doctrine of the ministry held little appeal for them. Moreover, by that time political thinking had become very much more sophisticated. Systems of ecclesiastical government were devised with the same elaboration as secular forms of government.

The twentieth-century church would have as little sympathy as that of the sixteenth with Cyprian's teaching about the ministry. Modern Christians would shrink from restricting the power of the Spirit within the boundaries of the church or from defining the church as the one place of safety in an evil and dissolving world. But modern Christians have also become disenchanted with complex and elaborate institutional forms. We do hope for some form of church which can be clearly and visibly one, organically one, in the sense of being a single living organism. This is one of the themes of *De Unitate* with its picture of the dynamic, proliferating, exuberant church. We also respond sympathetically to Cyprian's concept of a unity derived from personal relationships: a bishop's love for his own flock and his love for his brother bishops. Perhaps there may be the opportunity now, as there was not in Cyprian's own day, to translate this into actual practice, whether or not we use the term 'bishop' for this relationship.

9

STEPHEN died in the August of 257. For Cyprian this cannot have been anything other than a relief, for it is obvious that the quarrel had hit hard. Valerian's edict had, moreover, made persecution a reality once more, and the controversy between the two bishops was dissipating the church's strength at a time when it was desperately needed to resist the pressure from without.

The story goes that Valerian at first favoured Christianity. The very uprightness of character that had made Decius choose him as censor would attract Christians also. There were many Christians in the imperial household and at first no sort of penalty was inflicted on them.[1] It seems likely that this is the real foundation for the tradition that Valerian was sympathetic to Christianity. There is no clear evidence that he was in any sense a potential convert.

The legend further goes on to say that it was Valerian's minister, Macrianus,[2] who was really responsible for the bitterly anti-Christian feeling and policy which developed as the empire suffered various disasters. Valerian marched eastwards to meet threats on the frontier. With the reins of government in Macrianus's hands and the unity and stability of the empire threatened from many different quarters, it is not really surprising that another attempt should be made to compel the Christians to abandon their exclusiveness in religion, and their tightly knit 'in-group' attitudes within society as a whole. Macrianus issued an edict of Valerian's which decreed that the leaders of the church should be sent into exile, that gatherings for Christian worship should cease and that Christians should no longer visit the cemeteries where they had been able to own property and to erect shrines for their dead and thus, in effect, establish liturgical centres with some semblance of legality.[3] The edict would make the business of the Christian church awkward and difficult. Compared with the savagery of Decius' campaign it was a most mild and moderate measure. It was aimed 'not at the Christian religion but at the Christian church'.[4] In other words, it was the order and organization of the church which was to be destroyed. If Decius had hoped to terrify and torture men and women into apostasy, Valerian and Macrianus hoped to throw the church into such a state of chaos that Christianity would fade away almost of its own accord.

Cyprian cared deeply for precisely those things which were chiefly threatened by the new policies. Order, discipline, authority and proper organization were the very substance of nearly every major issue in which he had been involved since he had first become a bishop. He had not long to wait before the terms of the edict were directly applied to himself. He was summoned to appear before the proconsul of Africa, Aspasius Paternus, on 30 August 257. The trial took place in the proconsul's *secretarium,* not in the public basilica. The proceedings were short and formal, since the facts were not in dispute, and the punishment was inevitable.

The proconsul began by citing the edict requiring that everyone should conform to the traditional religion of Rome. He had, presumably in terms of the clause against the bishops, been making inquiries 'about your name'.[5] 'I am', said Cyprian, 'a Christian and the Bishop. I know no gods other than the one, true God, who made heaven and earth, the sea and everything that is in them. This God we Christians serve: to him we pray, day and night, for ourselves, for all men, and for the safety of the Emperors [Valerian and Gallienus] themselves.' (Gallienus was Valerian's son and had been associated with his father in government and given particular responsibility for the western part of the empire.)

'You are, therefore, persisting in this mind?'

'A good mind, which knows God, it is not possible to change.'

'Will it be *possible* for you, then, to go into exile to the city of Curubis, in accordance with the instruction of Valerian and Gallienus?'

'I go.'

But Paternus had not finished. He had been instructed to take action against presbyters as well as bishops.

'Therefore I want to know from you who the presbyters are in this city.'

'You have well and usefully provided by your own laws that there are to be no informers. Therefore it is not possible for me to reveal and delate [the presbyters]. You will find them in their cities.'

'I am asking here and now.'

'Since discipline forbids that anyone should give himself up voluntarily, and this would also infringe your own regulations, it is not possible for them to give themselves up; but if they are sought by you, they can be found.'

'They will be found by me.'

Paternus went on to explain that Christian assemblies were forbidden and that the cemeteries were out of bounds. If these regulations were not obeyed, those who infringed them would be executed. Cyprian replied that the proconsul must do as he was told. The formal sentence of exile was then pronounced upon the bishop.

The former rhetorician could compliment himself on holding his own with the proconsul, picking up and playing on certain words, knowing which laws he could most usefully cite to his own advantage, and maintaining the same sarcastic formality which the governor himself chose to use. But if this was some small comfort, nothing could alter the fact that the bishop was being separated from his people and that the citizen of Carthage was being sent into exile. There would be no one to deal with the inevitable dislocation resulting from the prohibition of Christian worship, no one to hold the whole of the local church together. He had a fortnight in which to set God's house and his own in order.

In the dying summer Cyprian set off for Curubis. Pontius, the deacon, went with him. His road took him southward from

Carthage, over the low-lying, swampy, unhealthy country by the lake of Tunis, and then to the east across the peninsula of Cap Bon, out of sight of his own city, to the further coastline where Curubis stood with its back to Carthage and its face towards Asia Minor across the Mediterranean. In actual mileage it was no great distance from the capital city. Curubis itself was pleasant enough and the climate was good. His friends came out from Carthage to see him and the local people were kind to him.[6] Cyprian's case was far less unpleasant than that of some of the Numidian bishops who were sent to the salt mines. But it was frustrating all the same.

Inevitably, being Cyprian, the exiled bishop found a sum of money to send to his colleagues in the mines to help soften some of the harshness of their situation. Behind the rhetorician's flourishes of the letter[7] he wrote to them, one can detect depth of real emotion. He is irked by the restrictions placed upon him. He is proud that he has been exiled for confessing Christ. Yet he envies the Numidian bishops the glory they have earned by their greater sufferings. They are almost martyrs already. They may die for the Lord at any moment. Almost pathetically he writes,

> Because your word is more effective in prayer and because supplication in suffering obtains what it asks for more quickly, seek urgently and ask that God's mercy will complete the confession for us all, that from this darkness and these snares of the world God will set us free with you, whole and glorious; that we who are one here in the bond of love and peace, who have stood together against the injuries of the heretics and the oppressions of the heathen, may rejoice together in the heavenly kingdom.[8]

There was one great comfort. Cyprian had hardly been sentenced when a new bishop was chosen by the church in Rome, the fifth during the ten years that Cyprian himself had been in office. Sixtus was described from Cyprian's side as 'a good and peaceful bishop',[9] and the threatening schism between Rome and Carthage was prevented. The debate about re-baptism continued, and Dionysius of Alexandria, in particular, kept up a correspondence with the church at Rome and his new colleague there, maintaining vigorously the point of view of Africa and the east.[10] But with the death of Stephen much of the bitterness and acerbity had gone out of the controversy. No

Here, in the place he loved so much, with his own people and friends about him, he waited for the next move. He had the opportunity to escape for he was offered a choice of several hiding places by rich and influential friends. But this time Cyprian had either grown tired of prolonging the issue or else he judged that he could serve God and the church better by martyrdom than by going into hiding as he had done in the first persecution.

One begins to detect in Cyprian's words and actions an attitude of mind which it is extremely difficult to define without appearing cynical. There is an element of what looks like self-dramatization which gets stronger and stronger as the climax gets nearer. It is not simply a dramatic flavour which Pontius and other narrators have imposed upon their accounts of what happened, because it appears in what Cyprian wrote himself. It is as though he saw that there was a great role of heroic proportions which he had to play and was determined to do it justice. But this is not in the least to say or imply that he was insincere. When T. S. Eliot set out to make his study of martyrdom in *Murder in the Cathedral* he allowed precisely the same element to appear in Becket's sermon and in the final preparations for the murder. The archbishop is, in a very real sense, stage-managing his own martyrdom. This Cyprian, too, seems to have been determined to do.

He was, for one thing, determined to die in his own city and among his own people. Everything he had said about the bishop as the centre and focus of the church's life was to be translated into action in his death. The offers of help he had received allowed him to retain the initiative in his own hands. He would choose where and when to die. Galerius the proconsul was at Utica, twenty-five miles to the west. He sent officials to fetch Cyprian from his garden home, but the bishop had disappeared. It must have looked as if he had run away again after all and, no doubt, one of the reasons for the dramatic emphasis which Cyprian began to lay upon his martyrdom was his anxiety to prove himself. He must have felt sure of himself, that he would not deny his Lord when the moment came. He wrote to his people, giving them a calm and dignified explanation for his disappearance:

. . . I had been persuaded by the advice of my closest friends

to withdraw from my gardens for a time and I agreed
because a valid reason was given; the reason was that it is
proper for a bishop to confess the Lord in the city in which
he presides over the Church of the Lord, and that the whole
people should be glorified by their prelate's confession in their
presence. For whatever the bishop and confessor speaks in
that moment of confession, he speaks by inspiration of God
and as the mouthpiece of all.[15]

He waits, he tells them, for the return of the proconsul, praying
to be martyred amongst them. When Galerius gets back he will
come out of hiding to be sentenced and so say what the Lord
commands him to say. This insistence upon the martyr's dying
prophecy is, no doubt, a reflection of Matthew 10:19, 'When
they deliver you up, do not be anxious how you are to speak or
what you are to say; for what you are to say will be given you in
that hour; for it is not you who speak, but the Spirit of your
Father speaking through you.'[16] The whole passage was of
special significance to Cyprian. Three verses later comes the
saying, 'When they persecute you in one town flee to the next.'
This might be regarded as his guiding text in the first
persecution. He now looked forward to a fulfilment of the other
verse, prophetic inspiration at the moment of martyrdom. The
verses in between, 'He who endures to the end shall be saved,'
recurs in many of his letters[17] and is, in a very real sense, the
keynote of his *Exhortation to Martyrdom*.

But Cyprian was always the pastor, concerned for his people
and not merely wrapped up in himself. The very reason why he
longed to be martyred in Carthage and not in Utica was that it
would glorify and encourage his own flock. This concern comes
out in his final letter to them. When he has explained why he has
temporarily gone into hiding he goes on to tell them to keep
calm and quiet, not to stir up trouble for each other, nor to go
rashly into martyrdom. His last words to his people were, 'May
our Lord make you to remain safe in his Church, most loved
brothers, and may he stoop to preserve you. Let it be so, by His
mercy.'

Galerius returned to his capital towards the middle of
September. Cyprian emerged from hiding, true to his word, and
was at home again. On 13 September two senior officers were
sent early in the morning to seize him.[18] The proconsul was

outside the city in a garden residence called Sexti. There Cyprian was taken, but Galerius was apparently not well enough to deal with the case and it was remanded to the next day. The bishop was not allowed to return to his own home or gardens. He had to make the journey back into the city itself and was kept for the night in the house of one of the officers, where he was well treated and not too strictly imprisoned.

But rumours began to be heard through the town that Cyprian was to be tried. Crowds gathered about the house where he was. Pontius says they were well disposed to the prisoner, not (as on previous occasions) baying for his blood. His friends were allowed in to keep him company. The congregation kept a close watch outside so that they should not miss anything if action were taken surreptitiously. When morning came, it was hot and clear and brilliant. On foot Cyprian started the journey back to Sexti and the proconsul. But the crowds went, too, turning the whole thing into a triumphal procession. They went out of the city, across the athletes' race track, and at last came to the praetorium. Cyprian was soaked with sweat. He sat down to wait—and Pontius was quick to notice that the seat was covered with linen as a bishop's liturgical throne should be. One of the officers suggested (out of kindness or, perhaps, because he hoped to sell relics afterwards) that Cyprian might like to change his clothes. The bishop could not resist a macabre joke. Was it worth trying to cure discomforts which would probably be ended altogether that day?

Then the case was called. Proceedings were even shorter and more formal than on the previous occasion.

'You are Thascius Cyprianus?'

'I am.'

'You have allowed yourself to be the "father" [papa: pope] to persons of sacrilegious views?'

'I have.'

'The most sacred Emperors have commanded you to perform the rites.'

'I will not.'

The proconsul turned to the members of his council to ascertain their judgment. Then, briefly, he summed up the whole case:

'You have for a long time lived a wrong-headed life, and

have associated with many others in a criminal conspiracy. You have also set yourself up as an enemy of the Roman gods and the holy laws. Nor have the pious and most sacred princes, Valerian and Gallienus, the Emperors, and the most noble Valerian, the Caesar, been able to call you back to the performance of their own rites. And because you have been clearly proved to be the author and leader of gross crimes you will therefore in your own person be made an example for those whom you have by your own guilt associated with you. Discipline will be confirmed by your blood.'

Then he read the formal sentence from his tablet. It was exactly one year to the day, if Pontius can be believed, since Cyprian's dream at Curubus.

'It is our will that Thascius Cyprianus be put to death by the sword.'

There had been none of the sarcastic by-play of the earlier trial before Paternus. Galerius was ill and not anxious to prolong the matter. Cyprian had been dwelling upon the thought that he was not to plan and scheme for clever things to say, but was to wait for the Spirit to speak through him. When the words came they were short and simple, more impressive than the longest and most vivid prophesying. Cyprian the bishop said, 'Thank God!'

The contrast between Cyprian's behaviour at his first trial and at his second is important. It marks the final stage in the development of his personality and is related to the dramatic character which his life seems to acquire in the last few weeks before his martyrdom. Again it is unlikely that the sharp contrast is something which has been invented by those who recorded the scene. One would have expected from them a heightening of the flamboyance rather than the simplicity and directness which now characterized Cyprian. There is none of the pomposity of his early days as a bishop, none of the crackling sharpness of the controversialist. Cyprian has, quite simply, become a better person. It is this that gives his martyrdom its true and perfect touch of drama. It is this that makes the drama seem sincere rather than contrived.

In some of the things he wrote during his final exile at Curubis one can see him beginning to shoulder the role of the martyr already. This is not to say that he is simply acting a part. Other Christian martyrs, from St Paul at one end of the church's

Vienna Corpus & Oxford	Migne PL	Ante-Nicene Library
LXXIII	LXXIII	LXXII
LXXIV	LXXIV	LXXIII
LXXV	LXXV	LXXIV
LXXVI	LXXVII	LXXVI
LXXVII	LXXVIII	LXXVII
LXXVIII	LXXIX	LXXVIII
LXXIX	LXXX	LXXIX
LXXX	LXXXII	LXXXI
LXXXI	LXXXIII	LXXII

Epistle I in Ante-Nicene Christian Library and Migne is printed as the treatise *Ad Donatum* in CSEL and the Oxford edition.

The numbering of the paragraphs within each epistle differs slightly as between CSEL and Oxford.

Notes

Chapter 1

1. Pontius, *De Vita et Passione S. Cypriani,* xix. The rest of this chapter is based on facts or hints contained in the *Acta Proconsularia S. Cypriani,* and on some first-hand knowledge of Carthage and its environs. See also V. Saxer, *Vie liturgique et quotidienne à Carthage,* Pontifico Institutio di Archeologia Cristiana, 1969, pp. 303f.

Chapter 2

1. See e.g. R. Oliver and J. D. Page, *A Short History of Africa,* Penguin, Harmondsworth, 1962, pp. 60ff.
2. A. Graham, *Roman Africa,* Longmans Green, 1902, p. 2.
3. R. Bosworth Smith, *Carthage and the Carthaginians,* Longmans Green, 1894, p. 17.
4. Frend, pp. 78ff.
5. See B. H. Warmington, *Carthage,* Robert Hale, revised edition 1969, pp. 133f.
6. See E. S. Bouchier, *Life and Letters in Roman Africa,* Blackwell, Oxford, 1913, p. 14.
7. For the government and administration of Roman Africa, see Graham, *Roman Africa,* pp. 32ff.

8. See e.g. Frend, pp. 28ff., 38f., 58, 92.
9. Frend, p. 35.
10. Frend, pp. 57ff.
11. B. C. Dietrich, 'The Golden Art of Apuleius', *Greece and Rome*, vol. xiii, p. 203.
12. *The Apologia and Florida of Apuleius of Madaura* (tr. H. E. Butler), Clarendon Press, Oxford, 1909, p. 191. For a discussion of the possible influence of Apuleius on Cyprian, see H. Koch, *Cyprianische Untersuchungen*, Arbeiten zur Kirchengeschichte, Bonn, 1926, pp. 314–33.
13. *Confessions*, III, i, 1.
14. For some fascinating examples, see Warmington, *Carthage*, pp. 238ff.
15. G. and C. Charles-Picard, *Daily Life in Carthage in the Time of Hannibal*, (tr. A. E. Foster), Allen and Unwin, 1961, p. 151.
16. *Apologia*, 1; cf. xl.
17. Warmington, *Carthage*, p. 239.
18. Frend, p. 77.
19. Frend, p. 79.
20. Charles-Picard, *Daily Life in Carthage in the Time of Hannibal*, p. 79.
21. Frend, p. 79.
22. Frend, pp. 80ff.; cf. Charles-Picard, *Daily Life in Carthage in the Time of Hannibal*, pp. 43f.
23. Frend, p. 80.
24. *Apologia*, ix.
25. Charles-Picard, *Daily Life in Carthage in the Time of Hannibal*, pp. 43f.
26. *The Golden Ass by Lucius Apuleius* (tr. R. Graves), Penguin Books, Harmondsworth, 1958, p. 267.
27. Charles-Picard, *Daily Life in Carthage in the Time of Hannibal*, p. 64.
28. Charles-Picard, *Daily Life in Carthage in the Time of Hannibal*, p. 77.
29. See e.g. Frend, pp. 77ff. and 97ff., and the same author's *Martyrdom and Persecution in the Early Church*, Blackwell, Oxford, 1965, pp. 360ff. Cf. R. A. Markus, 'Christianity and Dissent in Roman North Africa', *Studies in Church History*, vol. IX, Cambridge, 1972, pp. 21ff.
30. As, for instance, that the first missionaries came from Rome. See Tertullian, *De Praescriptione*, xxxvi.
31. For Tertullian's life, see T. D. Barnes, *Tertullian: A Historical and Literary Study*, Clarendon Press, Oxford, 1971.
32. Quoted in J. Stevenson, *A New Eusebius*, SPCK, 1957, pp. 186.

42. R. L. Wilken, 'Toward a Social Interpretation of Early Christian Apologetics', *Church History*, vol. XXXIX, no. 4, pp. 437ff., suggests that Tertullian attempted to take this line, but at the same time implies that most educated men found Christianity unattractive.
43. W. H. C. Frend, 'Heresy and schism as social and national movements', *Studies in Church History*, IX, Cambridge University Press, 1972, pp. 41f.
44. Nagayam, *The Carthaginian Clergy during the Episcopate of Cyprian*, pp. 17ff. has a section devoted to the social status of the clergy, but has been able to glean surprisingly little information. Frend, p. 91, has some information about the lack of education among the clergy.
45. Frend, 'Heresy and schism as social and national movements', *Studies in Church History*, IX, p. 42.
46. L. S. Mazzolani, *The Idea of the City in Roman Thought* (tr. S. O'Donnell), Hollis and Carter, 1970, pp. 191, 205, 329ff.
47. See D. E. Groh, 'Tertullian's Polemic against Social Co-optation', *Church History*, vol. XL, pp. 7f., for a study of Tertullian's rejection of the Roman idea of *gloria*.
48. But see the suggestion made by G. Bardy, *The Christian Latin Literature of the First Six Centuries*, Catholic Library of Religious Knowledge, 1930, that Cyprian only abandoned the 'bombastic' literary style at some point *after* he had become a Christian. Perhaps the process of rejection took some little while to complete.
49. *Testimonium*, III, xcviii.
50. *Ad Donatum*, iv (somewhat paraphrased).
51. See above, p. 18. I am indebted, on this point as on several others in this section, to the Reverend Professor G. D. Kilpatrick of the Queen's College, Oxford.
52. R. D. Sider, *Ancient Rhetoric and the Art of Tertullian*, p. 2.
53. Ackroyd and Evans (eds.), *Cambridge History of the Bible*, pp. 345f., 425, 545.
54. Ackroyd and Evans (eds.), *Cambridge History of the Bible*, p. 545, and cf. Bardy, *The Christian Latin Literature of the First Six Centuries*, p. 167.
55. See M. F. Wiles, 'The Theological Legacy of St Cyprian', *Journal of Ecclesiastical History*, vol. XIV, pp. 139ff., and M. A. Fahey, *Cyprian and the Bible: a Study in Third-Century Exegesis*, Mohr, Tübingen, 1971, esp. pp. 46ff.
56. Wiles, 'The Theological Legacy of St Cyprian', p. 141, and G. S. M. Walker, *The Churchmanship of St Cyprian*, Lutterworth, 1968, p. 11.

Chapter 4

1. Pontius, *De Vita et Passione*, v.
2. See the lengthy discussion of the canonicity of the election in Benson, pp. 25ff. Benson probably assumes a far more formal concept of canonicity than was really current in the third century.
3. Frend, pp. 113f.
4. Cyprian, Ep XLIII, 1. See Nayagam, *The Carthaginian Clergy during the Episcopate of Cyprian*, pp. 70ff., for convenient short biographies of Cyprian's clergy.
5. Nagayam, *The Carthaginian Clergy during the Episcopate of Cyprian*, pp. 49f., points out that we know of 12 priests, 6 deacons and 7 subdeacons in Cyprian's Carthage, but proceeds to assert, without any real evidence, that the total numbers were probably double those.
6. Ep LXIII, for instance, suggests that Cyprian had been given fairly precise instruction.
7. Ep LIX, 6.
8. See e.g. Ep III, 3. I am not convinced by the argument that this epistle could only have been written after 253 (see R. E. Wallis, *The Writings of Cyprian*, Ante-Nicene Christian Library, VIII, T. and T. Clark, 1868, p. xi). It is entirely possible that Rogatianus said, almost in passing, to his new episcopal brother, 'What does one do about a contumacious deacon?' and was somewhat surprised to receive a theological treatise on discipline and obedience in reply. Cyprian was like that.
9. *De Habitu Virginis*, xxi.
10. *De Habitu Virginis*, xix.
11. *De Habitu Virginis*, xxi.
12. See Kidd, *History of the Church to A.D. 461*, vol. I, p. 430.
13. Ep XI, 4.
14. Ep LXIII, 16: the whole epistle is valuable for information about the celebration of the eucharist.
15. Archdale King, *The Liturgy of the Roman Church*, Longmans Green, 1965, *passim*, has a good deal of information about the third-century western liturgy and about what is known of African practice.
16. Ackroyd and Evans (eds.), *Cambridge History of the Bible*, p. 577.
17. For portable cathedra and table, see Davies, *The Origin and Development of Early Christian Architecture*, p. 94, and M. Deansely, 'Dura Europos', *Church Quarterly Review*, vol. CLXVIII, p. 10.
18. Saxer, *Vie liturgique et quotidienne à Carthage*, p. 194.

19. H. M. Gwatkin, *Early Church History*, Macmillan, 1909, vol. II, pp. 267ff., 283, argues that this is Cyprian's view.
20. Ep LXIII, 13.
21. Ep LXIII, 11.
22. But Professor G. D. Kilpatrick has pointed out to me that no certificates have been found at Doura-Europos.
23. *De Lapsis,* viii, ix.
24. Ep LIX, 6.
25. *Ad Donatum,* vii.
26. See below, p. 73.
27. Ep LII, 2.
28. Frend, p. 33.
29. Lebreton and Zeiller, *History of the Early Church,* Book III, p. 274, and cf. Benson, pp. 88, 120ff.
30. Ackroyd and Evans (eds.), *Cambridge History of the Bible,* p. 425.
31. Ep VIII.
32. Ep IX, 2.
33. Ep XXX, 1.
34. Ep XXIV.
35. Benson, p. 107.
36. Ep XLV, 1.
37. Ep V, 1.
38. Ep V, and Epp X, XIV, 2.
39. Ep V, 2.
40. Ep XI, 3.
41. Ep XI, esp. 8.
42. Ep XI, 6.
43. Ep XIV, 3.

Chapter 5

1. Caldonius' letter to Cyprian (Ep XXIV) seems to imply that Caldonius thinks Cyprian is still in Carthage and was, therefore, probably written before the news of his flight was public knowledge. Cyprian's reply (Ep XXV) speaks of five other letters on the subject which he has written and it is likely that these are Epp XV–XIX, which must also then be of an early date, even if Cyprian's reply to Calconius was delayed. Cyprian also speaks of a book (*libellum*) on the subject which he has written. This seems very early for his treatise *De Lapsis*. On the other hand Cyprian would hardly have been writing in this way to Caldonius after the latter had become one of his deputies. Perhaps the 'book' was an early recension of *De Lapsis*.

2. On the ambivalent attitude to Tertullian that Cyprian adopted, see M. Bévenot, *Cyprian: De Lapsis and De Ecclesiae Catholicae Unitate,* Clarendon Press, 1971, p. xvii.

3. Even Gwatkin, *Early Church History,* vol. II, p. 287f., who is in many ways a harsh critic of Cyprian's theology of church and ministry, argues that in practice, in the matter of the power to dispense God's forgiveness, Cyprian had to depart from his usual viewpoint.

4. Ep XVI, 2. See also Saxer, *Vie liturgique et quotidienne à Carthage,* pp. 145ff., for the North African penitential discipline of the time.

5. Ep XV.

6. See above, pp. 50 and 141.

7. Ep XXV.

8. Ep XXIII.

9. *Hanc formam.*

10. Epp XXI and XXII.

11. See Ep XXXVII, 1.

12. Ep XXVI.

13. Ep XXVII, 2.

14. Ep XXVII, 1.

15. Ep XXVII.

16. See Ep XXX, 5.

17. Ep XXXV.

18. Ep XXXIV, 1.

19. E.g. his directions to the lapsed in Ep XXXIII.

20. Ep XLIII, 5.

21. Ep XIV, 4.

22. Ep XXXIII, 1.

23. Ep XLIII, 4.

24. For the date of *De Opere et Eleemosynis,* see Fahey, *Cyprian and the the Bible: A Study in Third-Century Exegesis,* p. 20. For Cyprian's views on almsgiving, see Ackroyd and Evans (eds.), *Cambridge History of the Bible,* p. 425. J. A. Burnaby, *Amor Dei,* Hodder and Stoughton, 1938, pp. 133, 237, 255, has some very harsh things to say about Cyprian's teaching.

25. This was brought home to me quite sharply because just at the time when I was considering Burnaby's strictures on Cyprian (see n. 24), I was also taking a non-Christian pupil through the Gospels for the first time. He was plainly appalled by the contrast between what seemed to him to be the attempt at a disinterested morality found in Rabbinic literature and the tremendous emphasis upon a rewards-and-punishments morality in the Gospels.

26. Epp XVIII, 1, and XIX, 2.

27. See Stevenson, *A New Eusebius*, p. 228, where two examples are given. A third is printed in R. H. Bainton, *Early Christianity,* Van Nostrand, 1960, p. 89.
28. Ep XX, 2.
29. Ep XXI, 3.
30. This is, at least, a possible reading, implying that smoke was used to increase the terrible thirst. Ep XXII, 4.
31. Ep XX, 2.
32. *De Lapsis,* xxvii, somewhat freely translated.
33. See above, pp. 48ff.
34. Ep VIII, 3.
35. On the whole question of unforgivable sins, in relation to persecution and apostasy, see Frend, *Martyrdom and Persecution in the Early Church,* particularly pp. 45, 56, 79; see also pp. 389ff. on the Decian persecution.
36. Ep XXX.
37. Ep XXXI, 6; cf. Ep XXX, 4.
38. Ep XXXII.
39. Cf. Ep XXXIII, 2.

Chapter 6

1. E.g. Ep XVII, 3.
2. Epp IX, 3; X, 2.
3. Epp XVI, 1–2; XV, 1; XVII, 2.
4. Ep XIV, 4; cf. Ep XXXIV, 3.
5. Ep XIX, 2.
6. See above, p. 19.
7. See Frend, p. 49. The whole of chapters III and IV of Frend are useful on the character of the church of the African provinces. See also P. Monceaux, *Histoire Littéraire de l'Afrique chrétienne,* Leroux, Paris, 1902, vol. II, pp. 3ff, for information about the organization of and relationships between Mauretania and proconsular Africa.
8. Ep XLV, 2. *Plebs* in Cyprian's writings usually means the laity. He often speaks of his 'fellow-presbyters', so *fratres* may include others of the clergy besides the bishops. At any rate it is inconceivable that the clergy should have been excluded.
9. Ep XLV, 2.
10. See Benson, pp. 132ff.
11. Epp XLIV, 1; XLV, 1; LV, 8.
12. Ep XIX, 2.
13. Ep XLIV, 1.
14. Ep XLV, 4.

15. *De Lapsis,* i. M. Bévenot, *Cyprian: De Lapsis and De Ecclesiae Catholicae Unitate,* pp. xif., does not think that *De Lapsis* was addressed to the Council, and his opinion is a weighty one. Cf. also above, p. 141 (Chap. 5, n. 1.)
16. *De Lapsis,* vi. I have translated *in sacerdotibus* as 'in the bishops' because this is the sense in which Cyprian usually uses *sacerdos.*
17. *De Lapsis,* viii.
18. *De Lapsis,* ix.
19. See above, p. 64.
20. *De Lapsis,* xxix.
21. *De Lapsis,* xxxvi.
22. Ep LV.
23. Ep LV, 13.
24. Ep XLVII.
25. Ep XLIX.
26. Ep LIV, 1. The confessors' letter informing Cyprian of their decision is Ep LIII.
27. Ep LIV, 3.
28. Ep LII, 2.
29. Ep L.
30. See Kidd, *History of the Church to A.D. 461,* vol. I, pp. 459f.
31. Ep LXII.
32. Pontius, *De Vita et Passione,* ix.
33. Ep LVII, 2.
34. See above, p. 65.
35. Ep LVII.
36. Ep LIX, 10.
37. See e.g. Ep LXIV.
38. Ep LIX, 15.
39. Ep LIX, 11.
40. Ep LIX, 15.
41. Ep LIX, 15.

Chapter 7

1. Ep LXI.
2. See above, p. 31.
3. See above, p. 41.
4. Ep LIII, 2.
5. *De Habitu Virginis,* v.
6. Ep LIV, 2, 3.
7. Ep XLVIII, 1, 4.
8. Ep XLIX.
9. Ep LIX, 17.

10. Ep LXI, 4.
11. Ep LXVII, 6.
12. Ep LXVII, 5.
13. Ep LXVII, 3.
14. Ep LXVIII, 1. There is some doubt about the authenticity of this letter, but the style is like Cyprian's and it fits into the general pattern of events.
15. Ep LXVIII, 5.
16. Ep LXIX, 8; cf. Epp III, 1; LXVII, 1, 3, etc.
17. Cf. Wiles, 'The Theological Legacy of St. Cyprian', *Journal of Ecclesiastical History,* vol. XIV, no. 2, p. 145.
18. Ep LXIX, 10. Stephen is not mentioned by name.
19. Neither side would, of course, really recognize this as *re*baptism. Cyprian would say that schismatic baptism was not baptism, and that returned schismatics were being baptized for the first time. Stephen would say that their first baptism was valid and that they could not really be baptized again. On the specific question of the North African tradition, see Walker, *The Churchmanship of St. Cyprian,* p. 31.
20. Leaving aside the question whether the 'true' church here would mean the Montanists.
21. *De Baptismo,* xv.
22. Ep LXXI, 4, and see p. 19 above.
23. Ep LXXI, 3.
24. Ep LXXI, 3.
25. *De Bono Patientiae,* ix. Cf. *De Zelo et Livore,* xi.
26. I am indebted for this idea to M. Thurian, 'The Unity of the Ministry', *Church Quarterly Review,* vol. CLXII, pp. 299ff.
27. *De Zelo et Livore,* xviii.
28. Ep LXXIII, 1.
29. Ep LXXII, 3, slightly paraphrased.
30. Ep LXXIII.
31. See also p. 101 below.
32. Ep LXXIII, 21.
33. Ep LXXIII, 9; CF. 6 and 21.
34. Ep LXXIII, 7, 15; and see the treatment of the relationship between original sin, baptism and the lapsed in Cyprian's thought in J. Pelikan, *Development of Christian Doctrine,* Yale University Press, 1969, pp. 79ff.
35. See the passage quoted from Tertullian, above p. 18, and cf. Ep XXVII, 3, where Cyprian contrasts baptism in the name of the Trinity and forgiveness granted in the name of the confessors.
36. See e.g. Epp XVII, 2 and XV, 1.
37. Ep LXXI, 2.
38. Ep LXXIII, 6; cf. C. E. Pocknee, 'Confirmation and the

Reconciliation of Heretics and Apostates', *Church Quarterly Review,* vol. CLXVI, pp. 357ff.
39. Ep LXXV, 25.
40. Ep LXXV.
41. Ep LXXIV.
42. Ep LXXIV, 11.
43. *Sententiae Episcoporum*: PL III, 1052.
44. *Sententiae Episcoporum:* PL III, 1054.

Chapter 8

1. See below, p. 110.
2. See e.g. S. L. Greenslade, *Schism in the Early Church,* SCM, 1953, p. 170.
3. Kidd, *History of the Church to A.D. 461,* vol. I, p. 456.
4. The Latin is *tinctus*; I can think of no single English word that will convey the idea of a tainted baptism.
5. Ep LXX, 2. 'Bishop' is again in the original *sacerdos*.
6. H. von Campenhausen, *Ecclesiastical Authority and Spiritual Power in the Church of the First Three Centuries* (tr. J. A. Baker), A. and C. Black, 1969, pp. 265ff., believes Cyprian to be partly responsible for the substitution of secular concepts of authority for the original Christian idea of spiritual power. He is not unsympathetic to Cyprian but believes that on this point Cyprian was simply obeying the logic of political thinking— presumably the logic of the possible (p. 291).
7. Frend, p. 140. Even von Campenhausen, *Ecclesiastical Authority and Spiritual Power in the Church of the First Three Centuries,* pp. 272f., makes it very clear that Cyprian's thought attempts this fusion, though he is inclined to underplay the importance of spiritual forces in Cyprian's thinking and makes him too much the Roman jurist.
8. See above, p. 89.
9. See above, p. 17.
10. See above, p. 74.
11. See above, p. 89.
12. See above, p. 68.
13. See Lebreton and Zeiller, *A History of the Early Church,* Book III, p. 300.
14. Ep LXVIII, 5.
15. See above, p. 87.
16. Cf. Frend, p. 140.
17. See above, p. 72.

10. Eusebius, *Ecclesiastical History*, VII, v.
11. Pontius, *De Vita et Passione*, xii.
12. *De Exhortatione Martyrii*, xiii; and see also E. L. Hummel, *The Concept of Martyrdom according to St. Cyprian of Carthage*, Catholic University of America Press, 1946, *passim*.
13. Ep LXXX, 1.
14. This is Ep LXXX.
15. Ep LXXXI, 1.
16. Cf. Ep X, the story of Mappalicus.
17. E.g. Epp XII, 1, and XIV, 2.
18. This account of Cyprian's last days is based on Pontius' *Life* and the *Acta Proconsularia* in Migne, PL III, 1498ff.
19. *Ad Donatum*, vii.
20. See above, p. 16.
21. See M. F. Wiles, *The Christian Fathers*, Hodder and Stoughton, 1966, p. 131, and esp. R. M. Grant, *Augustus to Constantine*, Collins, 1971, p. 335.
22. *De Exhortatione Martyrii*, xiii.